# OECD Investment Policy Reviews

Caribbean Rim:
Costa Rica, Dominican Republic and Jamaica

OECD

ORGANISATION FOR ECONOMIC CO-OPERATION AND DEVELOPMENT

## ORGANISATION FOR ECONOMIC CO-OPERATION AND DEVELOPMENT

Pursuant to Article 1 of the Convention signed in Paris on 14th December 1960, and which came into force on 30th September 1961, the Organisation for Economic Co-operation and Development (OECD) shall promote policies designed:

- to achieve the highest sustainable economic growth and employment and a rising standard of living in member countries, while maintaining financial stability, and thus to contribute to the development of the world economy;
- to contribute to sound economic expansion in member as well as non-member countries in the process of economic development; and
- to contribute to the expansion of world trade on a multilateral, non-discriminatory basis in accordance with international obligations.

The original member countries of the OECD are Austria, Belgium, Canada, Denmark, France, Germany, Greece, Iceland, Ireland, Italy, Luxembourg, the Netherlands, Norway, Portugal, Spain, Sweden, Switzerland, Turkey, the United Kingdom and the United States. The following countries became members subsequently through accession at the dates indicated hereafter: Japan (28th April 1964), Finland (28th January 1969), Australia (7th June 1971), New Zealand (29th May 1973), Mexico (18th May 1994), the Czech Republic (21st December 1995), Hungary (7th May 1996), Poland (22nd November 1996), Korea (12th December 1996) and the Slovak Republic (14h December 2000). The Commission of the European Communities takes part in the work of the OECD (Article 13 of the OECD Convention).

## OECD CENTRE FOR CO-OPERATION WITH NON-MEMBERS

The OECD Centre for Co-operation with Non-Members (CCNM) promotes and co-ordinates OECD's policy dialogue and co-operation with economies outside the OECD area. The OECD currently maintains policy co-operation with approximately 70 non-member economies.

The essence of CCNM co-operative programmes with non-members is to make the rich and varied assets of the OECD available beyond its current membership to interested non-members. For example, the OECD's unique co-operative working methods that have been developed over many years; a stock of best practices across all areas of public policy experiences among members; on-going policy dialogue among senior representatives from capitals, reinforced by reciprocal peer pressure; and the capacity to address interdisciplinary issues. All of this is supported by a rich historical database and strong analytical capacity within the Secretariat. Likewise, member countries benefit from the exchange of experience with experts and officials from non-member economies.

The CCNM's programmes cover the major policy areas of OECD expertise that are of mutual interest to non-members. These include: economic monitoring, statistics, structural adjustment through sectoral policies, trade policy, international investment, financial sector reform, international taxation, environment, agriculture, labour market, education and social policy, as well as innovation and technological policy development.

*Publié en français sous le titre :*
**Examens de l'OCDE des politiques de l'investissement**
Série sur les Caraïbes : Costa Rica, République dominicaine et Jamaïque

© OECD 2004

# Foreword

*The Caribbean Rim Investment Initiative (CRII) is an effort promoted by the OECD, within the programme of work of its Centre for Co-operation with Non-Members (CCNM), to develop a creative and pragmatic co operative approach between countries of Central America and the Caribbean and other international organisations with a view to enhancing investment opportunities in the region.*

*Several reasons justify the focus on the countries of the Caribbean Basin. In addition to constituting a distinct geographic area, this region comprises more than half of the countries of the Americas and practically all of the smallest economies in the Hemisphere. Despite some common elements, the region does present a high degree of heterogeneity. It includes countries with just a few thousand inhabitants and others with cities of several million, societies with relatively high human development achievements while others endure the worst living conditions on the continent, some are strong democracies, other still have weak political institutions. Most of the striking contrasts in the Americas may be found in this region. The fact that the Caribbean Basin represents such a mosaic of economic, political and social diversity explains in part why this region has been less studied relatively to other regions in Latin America. However, this reality also points to the need to promote initiatives specifically tailored to address the complex realities of these countries.*

*The origins of the CRII can be traced back to two workshops held in the Dominican Republic in April 2000 and in Curaçao in April 2001, where government officials from Caribbean Basin countries, private sector participants, and representatives of the OECD and other international organisations exchanged views on how these economies could improve their investment climate, as a critical condition to promote economic development and fight poverty. The CRII is a concrete and tangible exercise to support Caribbean and Central American countries in their efforts to improve their investment climate, attract increasing flows of investment – both foreign and domestic – and maximise the benefits that their economies and societies may draw from such flows.*

*A peer review of these reports took place at the CRII meeting held in Kingston, Jamaica on 11 March 2003.*

*The reports will serve as a basis for developing an investment policy reform agenda which could qualify for support by bilateral and international organisations including the IDB.*

OECD INVESTMENT POLICY REVIEWS – ISBN 92-64-10509-3 – © OECD 2004

3

We wish to thank our donors (The Kingdom of the Netherlands, United Kingdom), co-sponsor, the Inter American Development Bank (IDB), the consultants (Maryse Robert and Roberto Echandi), our contact points (Patricia Francis, from Jamaica; Anabel Gonzalez and Irene Arguedas from Costa Rica and Elka Schecker from the Dominican Republic) as well as other organisations that provided technical advice such as the Economic Commission for Latin America and the Caribbean (ECLAC), the Caribbean Community (CARICOM) and the Organisation of American States (OAS).

The reports are published under the responsibility of the Secretary-General of the OECD.

Eric Burgeat
Director
Centre for Co-operation
with Non-Members

Rainer Geiger
Deputy Director
Directorate for Financial
and Enterprise Affairs

# Table of Contents

# Dominican Republic

Investors have identified export incentives, labour costs and worker productivity as strong factors attracting FDI to the Dominican Republic. A state of the art telecommunications infrastructure, political and macroeconomic stability and access to regional and global markets are identified by investors as key elements in attracting Foreign Direct Investment (FDI). The Dominican Government is committed to continuing market oriented reforms, strengthening the rule of law, investing in human capital and education and creating the proper conditions to attract FDI.

This report looks at areas where there have been marked improvements such as crime, taxes, regulations and the general "helpfulness" of the government to the business community. It also examines factors that still need to be addressed to improve the investment climate in the Dominican Republic and its ability to compete for higher value-added FDI.

OECD INVESTMENT POLICY REVIEWS – ISBN 92-64-10509-3 – © OECD 2004

# Preface

The Dominican Republic is proud to be part of the first group of countries that ventured in a new OECD project geared towards the Caribbean, the Caribbean Rim Investment Initiative.

In April 2000, we hosted in Santo Domingo the first workshop between the OECD and Caribbean States that resulted in the creation of a Steering Group to work closely in the design and implementation of a three-year cooperation programme to enhance investment opportunities in the region and seek ways to mobilise productive investment.

Now in your hands is one of the products of such collaboration. We contributed openly and honestly to this Business Environment Report (BER) with the sincere understanding that through this benchmarking exercise we can continue to improve our investment climate and to promote foreign direct investment.

The fast-paced and volatile post 9/11 economic environment may have already impacted some of the assessments made in this report. However, the Dominican Government remains committed to continuing market oriented reforms, strengthening the rule of law, investing in human capital and education, and creating the proper conditions to attract foreign direct investment.

Based on this BER we have launched, together with the OECD and the Inter American Development Bank, an Investment Policy Reform Agenda to address the issues raised by this study.

Finally, the Dominican business climate is enhanced by our democratic tradition, social and political stability, economic growth, preferential access to world markets, the kindness of our weather and our greatest asset of all, the Dominican people, which we invite you all to meet.

Danilo Del Rosario V.
Secretary of State
Center for Export and Investment
of the Dominican Republic (CEI-RD fka OPI-RD)

ISBN 92-64-10509-3
OECD Investment Policy Reviews
Caribbean Rim: Costa Rica, Dominican Republic and Jamaica
© OECD 2004

# Executive Summary

Located between the North Atlantic Ocean and the Caribbean Sea, on the island of Hispaniola, which it shares with Haiti, the Dominican Republic is a small country twice the size of the state of Massachusetts, with a population of 8.6 million people and a per capita income of US$2 500 in 2001.[1] After a decade characterized by an unprecedented annual growth rate exceeding 6 per cent, the highest such rate in Latin America and the Caribbean, and an increase of over US$4 billion in foreign direct investment (FDI) inflows, economic growth fell to 2.7 per cent in 2001 due in large part to the slowdown in the US economy, while FDI reached an impressive US$1.2 billion. The Dominican economy recovered in 2002 and grew at an estimated rate of 4.1 per cent. FDI inflows amounted to US$850 million.[2]

The country experienced a period of strong growth in the 1970s, which was followed in the early 1980s by a significant slowdown in production and severe balance-of-payments problems compounded by high import and export tariffs, domestic price controls as well as expansionary monetary and fiscal policies. Whereas the Dominican economy grew in the late 1980s, as a result of higher spending, inflation reached 80 per cent in 1990 and international reserves and income growth fell sharply. The Government then implemented a series of economic reforms aimed at reducing the budget deficit, curtailing money supply and devaluing the exchange rate, eliminating price controls and reducing the anti-export bias in the economy. These reforms initiated in 1991 were accompanied by others in areas such as labor, taxation, and the financial system. In 1995, the Foreign Investment Law liberalized the investment regime and abolished most barriers to national treatment.

The Dominican Republic is principally a services economy, albeit it has traditionally been known as an exporter of primary products such as mining, sugar, coffee, and tobacco. The services sector now accounts for over 55 per cent of the domestic output and is the largest employer in the country. Free trade zones (FTZs), tourism, telecommunications as well as construction are the core sectors of the economy.

FDI inflows are a necessary component in the development strategy of the Dominican Republic, and structural reforms implemented over the past decade have undoubtedly contributed to increase investor confidence and FDI levels. Foreign investors have principally been attracted to FTZs due to fiscal incentives and low labor cost, and to the communications, electricity, and tourism sectors. These sectors have generated higher economic growth and attracted higher levels of FDI than more traditional segments (agriculture, non-FTZ manufacturing, and financial services) of the Dominican economy. While considerable progress has been accomplished and the Dominican Republic remains one of the best performers in Latin America and the Caribbean, the country must continue to improve its business environment to sustain and increase the current investment trends.

The investment strategy of the Dominican Republic is based on a two-pronged approach aimed at promoting FDI in FTZs and in infrastructure services, including via the privatization of state-owned enterprises. Recognizing the significance of FDI for the FTZ sector, the Government has recently sought to attract foreign investors in high value-added mega projects, which go beyond the efficiency-seeking investment traditionally present in the FTZ sector. For instance, in February 2003, President Mejía announced that he had enlisted a new partner, *Dubai's Ports, Customs and Free Zone Corporation*, in a scheme to develop a port and free trade zone on the coast of Monte Cristi, in the north-western corner of the country, in what may become the largest single foreign investment in the Dominican Republic (US$4.1 billion). The Dubai firm has signed a 19-year concession to develop and manage a 30-square-kilometre FTZ, a port complex, a cargo airport and a passenger airport near the city of Monte Cristi. The proposed project will be developed in an area the size of a medium-sized city. It includes the modernization of the current port of Manzanillo, the construction of a container ship and cargo freight facility, 1 000 hotel rooms, a 400-ship full service marina, an industrial FTZ, an ecological park, an airport, urban development projects, potable water and sewage infrastructure, a 100-megawatt power plant, a waste recycling facility, and highways.

Another example is the Cyber Park of Santo Domingo, which is a public-private partnership aimed at fostering technology and innovation. Located near the Las Americas International Airport, the park, once fully developed, will include residential villas, a golf course, a spa, a medical centre, and a host of other high-end amenities. It is an all-inclusive facility providing the best office space and a host of supporting programs and infrastructure so that employees can live and work in the park. In 2002, the Cyber Park welcomed twelve firms specializing in data processing, data recovery, e-commerce, and also a number of call centres. A major feature of the park is the Las Americas Institute of Technology, a computer science training centre that houses its own research and development laboratories. The institute provides customized courses and training to park tenants as well as access to research facilities.

Successive governments have privatized numerous state-owned enterprises, which explains why very few government-owned enterprises remain in the Dominican Republic today.[3] The Dominican Government has recently sought to improve infrastructure services with a view to attracting more FDI. For example, in February 2003, President Mejía announced the construction of the San Pedro de Macoris-La Romana highway expansion. The Government entrusted the Spanish-Dominican engineering firm *Concesionaria Dominicana de Autopistas y Carreteras* with the 30-year concession contract. Construction time is estimated to take two years. The construction work at the Multimodal Terminal at Punta Caucedo has also advanced significantly, with partial operation of the country's first terminal of mega-ship capacity expected to begin by the end of 2003. The 50-hectare Caucedo Terminal will provide extensive container handling capability to and from the Dominican Republic. The port's location in the centre of North-South and East-West trade lanes is expected to competitively position the Caucedo port as a transhipment hub of the Caribbean. The country will also greatly benefit from lower freight rates. Currently, the cost of shipping a container from Santo Domingo to Miami is US$2 800, from Costa Rica to Miami it is US$2 000 and from Honduras, it amounts to US$1 800.

The country offers numerous opportunities to foreign investors. The process of further opening up the financial services sector to foreign investment, as allowed under the new Monetary and Financial Code, which became law in November 2002, is one such example. This will contribute to strengthen the efficiency and solvency of the Dominican financial system and create spillover effects in other sectors of the economy. Wholesale and retail trade as well as tourism facilities remain very strong sectors where foreign firms can invest and benefit and where strong backward linkages can be developed. The telecommunications industry with its modern and competitive regulatory framework also represents an excellent sector for future FDI. In fact, foreign companies, especially those from the United States, Canada and Spain, have been investing heavily in the telecommunications and energy sectors in recent years, where demand far exceeds supply. Traditional FTZs also remain very attractive, albeit export subsidy programs under the WTO Agreement on Subsidies and Countervailing Duties (SCM) are to be eliminated by the end of 2007.[4] The FTZ-based apparel sector could be adversely affected by preferences granted by the United States to Central American countries under the US-Central American Free Trade Agreement (CAFTA), whose negotiations were launched on January 8, 2003. However, overall trade liberalization within the Free Trade of the Americas (FTAA) process, in particular with rules of origin allowing for local value-added activities, would provide foreign investors in the Dominican Republic with additional market opportunities abroad and would offset the trade and investment diversion effects of such preferences.

Investor perceptions of the Dominican Republic as a location for investment are quite positive. The state-of-the-art telecommunications infrastructure, which is one of the most advanced systems in Latin America, openness to foreign investment, political and macroeconomic stability, and access to global and regional markets are factors identified by investors as the key elements contributing to attract FDI. The country's geographic location is also considered a major source of competitive advantage by export-oriented firms such as those located in FTZs, which regard the country's access to regional and global markets as a strategic element in choosing the Dominican Republic as a location for investment. These firms have identified export incentives and FTZs, labor costs and worker productivity as strong factors attracting FDI to the Dominican Republic. For firms, which are market-seeking, the size of the Dominican market is one important factor. Moreover, investors recognize that there have been marked improvements, in general, over the past few years in the areas of crime (both street and organized), taxes, regulations, and "helpfulness" of the Government to the business community.

Among factors that need to be improved, investors indicate the high cost of electricity and the shortage of skilled workers and supervisors. Foreign market-seeking firms located outside the FTZs identified the education level of workers as a major weakness. Both elements can be addressed with appropriate reforms and in securing the resources necessary to carry out such reforms. They would contribute to attract more FDI and would also clearly benefit domestic investors. The enactment of the Electricity Law in 2001 was an important step in improving the framework for a more competitive electricity sector but as demand for power in this fast-growing economy doubled over the past decade, increased investment is much needed in power generation capacity and in the overburdened transmission and distribution systems. With respect to the labor force, the increase in the skill level of the Dominican workforce, which is perceived by investors as being "competent, trainable and cooperative" would help the Dominican Republic to compete for higher value-added foreign direct investment.

Other factors affecting the Dominican Republic's competitiveness for investment are Government's regulations and taxes. It is worth noting that the Dominican Republic is one of the few Latin American countries, which has successfully implemented a comprehensive tax reform in recent years. While many other countries in the region had to abandon, postpone or scale back their reforms, the Dominican Republic adopted in 2000 a flat tax on fuel, raised the value-added tax (ITBIS) rate from 8 per cent to 12 per cent, and increased selective excise taxes on tobacco and alcohol, which have also contributed to raise tax receipts. The tax reform was accompanied by a tariff reform that slashed the number of tariffs by half and the maximum tariff from 35 per cent to 20 per cent.[5] However, in February 2003, the Government imposed by decree a 10 per cent surcharge on all imports – except food, medicines, raw materials and capital goods – for a period of 90 days, as part of a series of measures to promote austerity in an attempt to curb the depreciation of the exchange rate.

Tax changes implemented in 2000 have had a positive impact on compliance and have removed a number of distortions in the economy. But more remains to be done. For example, the phasing out of the 5 per cent commission on foreign-exchange transactions was delayed until October 2001, with a reduction of 0.25 percentage point. Under the new Monetary and Financial Code of November 2002, this exchange commission is to be eliminated within twelve months. The new Code, which strengthens the legal framework for investment in the country, also guarantees that the currency and interest rates will be determined by market forces, hence the currency will float freely and interest rates will no longer be set at a maximum of 12 per cent. The Code prohibits exchange controls and ensures that contracts signed in the country in a foreign currency will be regarded as legal. Moreover, the Code strengthens the autonomy of the Central Bank since, as of July 2004, it will no longer be possible for the Central Bank governor and Monetary Board members to be removed from their posts until the end of their two-year terms.

Efforts to liberalize the Dominican economy, invest in human capital and improve governance, fiscal transparency, and management need to be enhanced in the current decade to ensure that the country continues to enjoy strong growth and make further progress in reducing income inequality, which constitutes a serious problem since the poorest half of the population receives less than 20 per cent of national income, whereas the top 10 per cent captures slightly less than 40 per cent of the total.

The Dominican Republic is at a crossroads. In order to sustain economic growth, the country must continue to improve its business environment to attract FDI in FTZs and in infrastructure services (telecom, energy, financial services, and transport). It must also broaden the number of sectors that receive FDI and must especially encourage foreign investment in the non-FTZ manufacturing sectors of the economy. The country would particularly benefit from eliminating the remaining measures that create an anti-export bias in the domestically-oriented sectors of the Dominican economy and the cumbersome administrative procedures facing investors. Another key element is the quality of the labor force and the need to invest in training and re-training programs aimed at improving the productivity of the workforce.

On May 2003, Dominican authorities had to intervene in one of one country's largest private banks, the Banco Intercontinental, BANINTER, because of fraud. To avoid a domino effect, the Superintendency and the Central Bank had to address severe weaknesses in other two private banks, by means of substantial liquidity assistance. Thus, the *peso* depreciated and inflation increased in 2003, whiles the public sector debt – and the cost of servicing it – has risen considerably. This, combined with a deteriorating external environment (the war on Iraq and new security measures affecting tourism and trade), forced the DR Government to seek assistance from the International Monetary Fund.

The Executive Board of the International Monetary Fund (IMF) 29th August approved a two-year SDR 437.8 million (about US$600 million) Stand-By Arrangement for the Dominican Republic to support the country's economic program through August 2005.

The approval opens the way for the release of about US$120 million under the arrangement over the next 24 months. The IMF agreement is designed to strengthen the Dominican banking system, fortify public finances and frame consistent monetary and fiscal policies.

The government has prepared a comprehensive program to restore macroeconomic stability, maintain confidence in the banking system, ensure debt sustainability, and resume strong growth. Broad based social and political support is being secured for this effort.

Further consolidations of reforms that will continue to provide a sound business environment, such as the privatisation of the electricity sector and trade liberalisation, are also important policy initiatives in this area. Special attention is being given to provide adequate political and regulatory frameworks and institutional capacity to ensure a transparent, competitive and efficient environment which would benefit consumers and public finances alike.

Attention to the economic integration schemes is an important aspect of the economic policy of the Dominican Republic. Since 1997, when the first FTA with Central America was signed, the country has subscribed an FTA with CARICOM, in 1998. In addition, the integration strategy of the Dominican Republic has allowed for joint negotiations with Central America and CARICOM with OMC, the European Union and the Americas Free Trade Agreement (FTAA). Currently the country is undergoing negotiations for Free Trade Agreement with the United States.

Although the country faces numerous challenges in the coming years, within the next twelve months, a number of concrete measures could be implemented by the Government of the Dominican Republic, in the context of the National Competitiveness Plan launched in 2001 and with the support of international organisations such as the Inter-American Development Bank (IADB) and the Organization for Economic Cooperation and Development (OECD), to improve the investment climate in the country. These measures should include:

a) the enactment of a modern Commercial Code, which would eliminate the burdensome requirements for the establishment of a business;

b) the removal of administrative barriers with respect to land titling and registration, and customs administration;

c) the review of the incentive packages for investors, taking into account that the Dominican Republic may have to eliminate its export subsidy programs under the WTO Agreement on Subsidies and Countervailing Duties by the end of 2007 (unless WTO members agree on further postponement of the deadline to a later date). Such review should be undertaken using a cost-benefit analysis to assess the use and provision of these incentives in the country;

d) the establishment of an annual benchmark survey of investors views on critical issues affecting investment decisions; and

e) the establishment of a clearing house where small and medium-sized local companies meeting some well-defined standards of performance would register and could become suppliers of the foreign (and local) companies operating in FTZs. Such a mechanism would encourage backward linkages.

Reducing corruption is another issue that should continue to be addressed, as it imposes costs on firms. The announcement in early 2003 of the creation of a new department – *Fiscalia Anticorrupción* – as well as other government initiatives aimed at curbing corruption are welcomed steps.

ISBN 92-64-10509-3
OECD Investment Policy Reviews
Caribbean Rim: Costa Rica, Dominican Republic and Jamaica
© OECD 2004

# Chapter 1

# FDI Trends

## 1.1. Flows and stocks of FDI

FDI inflows into the Dominican Republic grew at a phenomenal average annual rate of 52 per cent from 1990 to 2000 (see Table 1.1). The first half of the decade was marked by a steady increase in FDI inflows and an average annual growth rate of 26.7 per cent. During the second half of the 1990s, in contrast, the country experienced declines and peaks, as well as more rapid growth in FDI inflows with an average annual rate of 77.6 per cent. The most severe reduction in inflows occurred in 1996 and might be explained by the adoption on 20 November 1995 of the Foreign Investment Law (No. 16-95), which eliminated restrictions on the repatriation of capital. A year later, inflows had regained the level reached in 1995. Moreover, the Government's privatization program, notably with respect to electricity services, and the reconstruction efforts that took place in the aftermath of Hurricane Georges in September 1998 help explain the 91 per cent rise in FDI inflows from 1998 to 1999.

Table 1.1. **FDI inflows, 1990-2001**

Millions of US dollars

|  | 1990 | 1991 | 1992 | 1993 | 1994 | 1995 | 1996 | 1997 | 1998 | 1999 | 2000 | 2001 |
|---|---|---|---|---|---|---|---|---|---|---|---|---|
| Total | 133 | 145 | 180 | 225 | 360 | 414.3 | 96.5 | 420.6 | 699.8 | 1 337.8 | 953.0 | 1 198 |

Source: UN Economic Commission for Latin America and the Caribbean, and Central Bank of the Dominican Republic.

In addition to traditional areas (mining, for example), services (such as electricity, telecommunications and tourism), as well as FTZs have greatly benefited from this influx of foreign capital in the 1990s. Services industries and efficiency-seeking investment in textiles, apparel and other sectors have attracted the bulk of FDI inflows into the Dominican Republic in recent years.

Table 1.2 shows that new investments have captured close to 60 per cent of all investment in the Dominican Republic between 1995 and 2000, whereas reinvestments account for only 38.5 per cent of the total, a lower share than other countries in the region such as Costa Rica for which reinvestments represented 53 per cent of total FDI in 2000. In December 2002, the Director of the Dominican Republic's Office for the Promotion of Investments (OPI-RD) announced that changes would be made to the Foreign Investment Law so as to provide incentives for the reinvestments of profits by foreign investors.

Table 1.2. **FDI inflows, 1995-2000**

Millions of US dollars

|  | New investment | Reinvestment | Other capital | Total |
|---|---|---|---|---|
| 1995 | 111.1 | 284.8 | 18.4 | 414.3 |
| 1996 | 75.6 | 69.7 | −48.8 | 96.5 |
| 1997 | 181.4 | 245.1 | −5.9 | 420.6 |
| 1998 | 293.5 | 343.7 | 32.6 | 669.8 |
| 1999 | 946.8 | 343.4 | 47.6 | 1 337.8 |
| 2000[1] | 658.4 | 210.8 | 83.8 | 953 |
| **Total** | **2 266.8** | **1 497.5** | **127.7** | **3 892** |

1. Preliminary data.

*Source:* International Department, Central Bank of the Dominican Republic.

Table 1.3. **FDI inward stock, 1990, 1995, 2000**

Millions of US dollars

|  | 1990 | 1995 | 2000 |
|---|---|---|---|
| **Total** | **572** | **1 707** | **5 214** |

*Source:* UNCTAD, World Investment Report 2002.

Table 1.3 indicates the extent to which FDI increased in the Dominican Republic during the last decade. The inward stock rose by an impressive factor of eight between 1990 and 2000.

Although data on FDI outflows is often anecdotic and not widely available, UNCTAD has estimated that Dominican investors abroad were particularly active in 1995 and 1996 where FDI outflows amounted to US$15 million and US$14 million, respectively (Table 1.4). In the recent past, Dominican companies have started investing abroad in major infrastructure service sectors. For example, the Dominican telecommunications company TRICOM is established in Panama and began operations in 2002 in Nicaragua. Moreover, the fertiliser company FERSAN is opening a plant in Jamaica, whereas Grupo Hormigones Moya plans to do the same in Costa Rica.

Table 1.4. **FDI outflows, 1995-2001**

Millions of US dollars

|  | 1995 | 1996 | 1997 | 1998 | 1999 | 2000 | 2001 |
|---|---|---|---|---|---|---|---|
| **Total** | **15** | **14** | **1** | **1** | **6** | **3** | **4** |

*Source:* UNCTAD, World Investment Report 2002.

## 1.2. Country of origin and destination

During the second half of the 1990s, Spain (26.2 per cent), the United States (21.2 per cent), and Canada (19.7 per cent) captured approximately 70 per cent of all FDI flows into the Dominican Republic. A few major sectors benefited from these investments: infrastructure services through the privatization of electricity and telecom services, tourism, retail trade, mining and export-oriented manufacturing industries (FTZs). While US FDI increased steadily during this period, Canadian inflows, in contrast, varied considerably from year to year. Moreover, investors from Grand Cayman, which is as part of the Cayman Islands a British dependency, have made significant investments into the Dominican Republic over the past six years. Also worth noting is the recent arrival of new foreign investors such as the French, the Chileans, and the Dutch. In fact, the percentage of FDI originating from Spain, the United States, and Canada decreased in relative terms in recent years. In 2000, for example, their combined share was of 55 per cent.[6]

Spain, whose total investments in the Dominican Republic surpass US$4 billion, is particularly active in tourism and the electricity distribution sector with Edenorte and Edesur owned by Union Fenosa. More recently, in November 2002, the Spanish group CITA identified the Dominican Republic as a strategic market in the Americas, and agreed to invest US$25 million in a cigar factory (La Tabacalera). The United States tops the list of the foreign investors with companies in sectors such as agribusiness, banking and finance, chemicals and pharmaceuticals, computer and data processing, consumer products, manufacturing and assembly, natural resources, telecom, and tourism and hospitality industry. Canada is principally present in mining and financial services. There are several Canadian firms doing business in the Dominican Republic, including Falconbridge, Placer Dome, Unigold, Vancouver Airport Services, Bell Helicopters, and Scotiabank.

At the end of 2002, French investments in the Dominican Republic were valued at US$400 million, with a concentration in beverages, mobile phone services, in addition to the Carrefour and Coforama stores on the eastern side of the Province of Santo Domingo, whereas German investments amounted to US$380 million. Italian investment is concentrated in FTZs and in shoe manufacturing with a new investment of US$40 million announced in June 2002.

British investment is more modest but growing. In February 2003, a British meat processing company made public that it will invest UK£9 million, over RD$ 250 million, in the construction of an industrial slaughterhouse in Santiago Rodríguez. This investment falls under Law 28-01, which provides incentives for investments on the border with Haiti. Another British company, the British American Tobacco Company (BAT), plans to invest US$35 million over the next five years.

OECD INVESTMENT POLICY REVIEWS – ISBN 92-64-10509-3 – © OECD 2004

Other key investors include *Dubai's Ports, Customs and Free Zone Corporation*, which is to manage a free-trade zone on the coast of Monte Cristi, in what could become the single largest foreign investment in the country (US$4.1 billion). New potential investors also comprise a business group from Morocco, who has plans to install a chain of eight Morocco handicraft stores in the Dominican Republic. The goods would be part of a US$8 million investment that also includes a manufacturing operation at a Dominican free zone. The announcement was made in May 2002, while President Mejía was touring Morocco.

Table 1.5. **FDI inflows by country of origin, 1995-2000**
Millions of US dollars and percentage

| | 1995 | 1996 | 1997 | 1998 | 1999 | 2000 | Total | Per cent |
|---|---|---|---|---|---|---|---|---|
| Spain | 60.8 | 61.2 | 52.4 | 205.6 | 457.1 | 190.1 | 1 027.2 | 26.2 |
| USA | 64.3 | 44.9 | 157.8 | 180.4 | 181.2 | 201.6 | 830.2 | 21.2 |
| Canada | 239.7 | −23.3 | 199.0 | 127.8 | 94.8 | 133.2 | 771.2 | 19.7 |
| Grand Cayman | 4.2 | 1.6 | 45.6 | 45.5 | 179.2 | 37.0 | 313.1 | 8.0 |
| England | 5.9 | 5.2 | 41.4 | 22.9 | 75.7 | 17.4 | 168.5 | 4.3 |
| France | – | – | – | – | 34.4 | 97.5 | 131.9 | 3.4 |
| Chile | – | – | – | – | 88.9 | 21.6 | 110.5 | 2.8 |
| Netherlands | – | – | – | – | 61.5 | 36.0 | 97.5 | 2.5 |
| Switzerland | 14.8 | 12.9 | 14.7 | 7.7 | 16.5 | 14.0 | 80.6 | 2.1 |
| Italy | – | – | 0.3 | 33.1 | 13.9 | 15.5 | 62.8 | 1.6 |
| Others | 24.6 | −6.0 | −90.6 | 76.8 | 134.6 | 189.0 | 328.4 | 8.4 |
| **Total** | **414.3** | **96.5** | **420.6** | **699.8** | **1 337.8** | **952.9** | **3 921.9** | **100** |

*Source:* Central Bank of the Dominican Republic.

## 1.3. Distribution by economic activity

The electricity sector through the Government's privatization program has been the main beneficiary of the influx of foreign capital into the Dominican Republic over the past three years (Table 1.6). While the sector accounted for only 7.7 per cent of total FDI in 1996, its share had risen to 47.2 per cent by 1999, when some of the thermoelectric plants and distribution facilities belonging to the public electricity company were privatized. Tourism also represents an important sector for FDI inflows into the country. New hotel facilities in recent years have been in part the result of the reconstruction efforts following Hurricane Georges in September 1998. Retail trade and telecom's shares of FDI are also significant.

The current trend points to the fact that infrastructure services (energy and telecom) have overtaken the export-oriented manufacturing sector and primary products as the lead category for FDI inflows. Although efficiency seeking-investment in FTZs, primarily in textile activities but also in tobacco, shoes,

Table 1.6. **FDI inflows by sector 1993-2000**
Millions of US dollars and percentage

| Sectors | 1993 | 1994 | 1995 | 1996 | 1997 | 1998 | 1999 | 2000[1] | Total | Per cent |
|---|---|---|---|---|---|---|---|---|---|---|
| Electricity | – | – | – | 7.5 | 42.9 | 33.4 | 631.4 | 281.9 | 997.1 | 25.4 |
| Tourism | 73.1 | 42.5 | 111.2 | 61.2 | 114.2 | 312.2 | 296.9 | 73.7 | 969.4 | 24.7 |
| Retail trade | 16.6 | 33.9 | 140.8 | 59.8 | 216.5 | 177.4 | 182.6 | 153.7 | 930.8 | 23.7 |
| Telecom | 93.1 | 123.7 | 149.3 | (36.2) | 32.8 | 117.1 | 98.0 | 272.2 | 633.2 | 16.1 |
| Fin. serv. | 6.5 | 6.7 | 13.0 | 4.2 | 14.2 | 29.5 | 40.9 | 45.3 | 147.1 | 3.8 |
| FTZs | – | – | – | – | – | – | 40.5 | 42.5 | 83.0 | 2.1 |
| Others | – | – | – | – | – | 30.2 | 47.6 | 83.7 | 161.5 | 4.1 |
| **Total** | **189.3** | **206.8** | **414.3** | **96.5** | **420.6** | **699.8** | **1 337.8** | **952.9** | **3 922** | **100.0** |

1. Preliminary data.
*Source:* Central Bank of the Dominican Republic.

electrical components, hospital supplies, and data processing remains important, the services industries account for more than 50 per cent of total FDI in the Dominican Republic. Infrastructure services – energy, telecom, financial services, transportation – are vital for the efficient operation of any economy. They play a major role in the competitiveness of all other sectors, including manufacturing and agriculture. Without well-functioning infrastructure services, a country cannot aspire to be competitive on the global scene.

## 1.4. Main foreign investors

The number of foreign investors into the Dominican Republic has also grown significantly in recent years. There are now over 500 foreign investors in the country. As Table 1.7 shows, the United States is home to seven of the ten largest investors in the Dominican Republic. These large investors are concentrated in telecommunications; sugar plantations; cigarettes, cigars and beer; mining; petroleum distribution; financial services; and household products. The electricity generation sector has also greatly benefited from an influx of FDI inflows. Firms operating in that sector rank 11th, 12th, 13th, 14th, and 16th among the largest investors in the country.[7]

## 1.5. Main explanatory factors for FDI

During the last decade, the Dominican Republic has eased restrictions on foreign direct investment and adopted policies aimed at attracting FDI flows in FTZs and in infrastructure services. Numerous elements, such as privatization initiatives, particularly in the non-hydroelectric power generation and distribution components of the national electricity company, the *Corporación Dominicana de Electricidad*, and the opening of state enterprises to private investment have contributed to the substantial increase in FDI inflows into the country.

Table 1.7. **The Dominican Republic's ten largest foreign investors**

| Company | Foreign investor/country of origin | Registered capital | Sector(s) |
|---|---|---|---|
| CODETEL[1] | Verizon (United States) | US$370 million | Telecommunications (phone service provider) |
| Central Romana Corporation[2] | United States | US$92 million | Sugar plantations (also: a mill, real estate, and a hotel) |
| E. León Jiménez, C.X.A. | A local partner of Phillip Morris (United States) | US$16.5 million | Cigarettes, cigars, and beer |
| Falconbridge Dominicana | Canada | US$15 million | Ferronickel production |
| Shell Company[3] | The Netherlands/England | US$14 million | Petroleum by-products distribution |
| CITIBANK | United States | US$13 million | Financial services (banking) |
| ESSO Standard Oil | United States | US$11 million | Petroleum by-products distribution |
| TEXACO Caribbean | United States | US$10 million | Petroleum by-products distribution |
| Colgate Palmolive[4] | United States | US$9.5 million | Household products |
| Bank of Nova Scotia | Canada | US$8 million | Financial services (banking) |

1. CODETEL is the Dominican Republic's main telephone provider. Incorporated in 1930, it has been a subsidiary of GTE for over two decades. As a result of the merger between GTE and Bell Atlantic in 2000, CODETEL is now controlled by Verizon.
2. Central Romana Corporation is the largest private sector employer in the country.
3. Shell operates the only petroleum refinery in the Dominican Republic.
4. Colgate Palmolive is the leading manufacturer of toothpaste in the country.
*Source:* OECD.

One key attraction of the Dominican Republic is the Cyber Park of Santo Domingo, which is a public-private partnership aimed at fostering technology and innovation. Located near the Las Americas International Airport, the park, once fully developed, will include residential villas, a golf course, a spa, a medical centre, and a host of other high-end amenities. It is an all-inclusive facility providing the best office space and a host of supporting programs and infrastructure so that employees can live and work in the park. In 2002, the Cyber Park welcomed twelve firms specializing in data processing, data recovery, e-commerce, and also a number of call centres. A major feature of the park is the Las Americas Institute of Technology, a computer science training centre that houses its own research and development laboratories. The institute provides customized courses and training to park tenants as well as access to research facilities.

### Market-seeking FDI in the Dominican Republic

In recent years, the Dominican Republic has benefited from a large influx of market-seeking FDI in services sectors, in particular in underdeveloped infrastructure services, which require large amounts of capital to operate and take advantage of economies of scale. For example, as demand for power in this fast-growing economy doubled in the past decade, numerous sectors, including tourist facilities, have had to invest heavily in their own private back-up generators. In 1999, the generation and distribution electricity sectors were part-privatized. A new Electricity Law (*Ley General de Electricidad*) enacted on July 27, 2001 provides for a modern regulatory framework and has helped alleviate numerous problems in the energy sector but increased investment in power generation capacity and in the transmission system are greatly needed to eliminate electricity shortages. The Electricity Law allows foreign investment in distribution and electricity generation with the exception of hydroelectricity. Transmission and hydroelectricity generation are reserved to the state. It is worth noting that power service in the Dominican Republic is the most expensive in the region.

In September 2002, Hong Kong-based Cavendish International made public that it would invest US$250 million to rehabilitate the Haina River sugar mill, which was one time the largest sugar mill in the world, and build another sugar mill in San Pedro de Macoris to produce alcohol. The company will purchase 1.6 million tons of sugar to produce ethanol, which will be mixed with gasoline and diesel. This is expected to cut 20 per cent off fuel costs in the Dominican Republic. Concurrently, with the signing of the project, President Mejía issued Decree 732-02, which establishes special economic and tax incentives for local and foreign companies investing in the production of ethanol and other bio-mass energy forms.

Telecom services have also registered significant increases in FDI. In 2002, the sector experienced a phenomenal increase in the first six months of the year drawing investments worth $106.5 million, up from $26.1 million in the first six months of 2001. The industry accounted for approximately 6.5 per cent of the Dominican GDP in 2001, up from 3.5 per cent in 1995.

Other market-seeking services sectors which have been the recipient of FDI inflows into the Dominican Republic include tourism and retail trade. Investments in the tourism sector rose by 57 per cent in the first six months of 2002.

## Natural resources-seeking FDI in the Dominican Republic

The Dominican Republic is very rich in minerals such as nickel, gold, silver, marble, limestone and granite. The mining sector has attracted a number of foreign companies. Falconbridge Dominicana, a Canadian-owned firm, operates a nickel mine and smelter, in which the Government has a 10-cent stake. Canadian gold giant Placer Dome has recently signed an agreement with the Government to take over the Pueblo Viejo gold-focused operation, which was operated by local state miner Rosario Dominicana until

OECD INVESTMENT POLICY REVIEWS – ISBN 92-64-10509-3 – © OECD 2004

environmental and minerals processing problems forced it to shut down in 1999. In April 2003, the Dominican Senate approved an amendment to the mining law in order to legalize the resumption of operations at the Pueblo Viejo gold mine in central Cotuí. Placer Dome, the Canadian company that currently holds the mining concession at Pueblo Viejo, has pledged to invest US\$336 million to reactivate the old Rosario mine, in addition to the sum of US\$1.5 million per year to be spent on water treatment.

In November 2002, Canada's Unigold Resources announced that it is investing US\$20-million dollars in the exploration of two potentially rich ore fields located in the Northwest region of the Dominican Republic. The two mining locations, Neíta and Sabaneta, are located in the provinces of Elias Piña, Dajabón and Santiago Rodriguez. Unigold is mainly looking for gold, silver, copper, and zinc.

The Mejía Government has spent a lot of efforts trying to attract FDI in mining. New legislation to make FDI in mining more investor-friendly is being considered. New regulations for non-metallic or industrial mining operations from *Semarena*, the country's environment and natural resources department, are designed to technically regulate the open-pit extraction of non-metallic materials such as limestone. These rules build on the existing regulations, such as a clause that refers specifically to methods used for drawing up environmental impact studies.

### Efficiency-seeking FDI in the Dominican Republic

Efficiency-seeking investment in the Dominican Republic is essentially concentrated in free trade zones (or *zonas francas*, as they as known in Spanish). The FTZ system began in 1969. It now has approximately 50 free zones with over 500 companies employing over 175 000 workers. The zones are regulated by Law 8-90 of January 15, 1990, which seeks to promote the establishment of new free zones and the growth of existing ones.

The range of FTZ production has increased markedly since 1969, when they were highly concentrated in textiles and clothing assembly. The sector stands to benefit from the Caribbean Basin Trade Partnership Act (CBTPA), which became effective October 1, 2000, and is an extension of the Caribbean Basin Initiative (CBI) implemented in 1984. The law is intended to restore advantages to the US's Caribbean and Central American trade partners equal to those enjoyed by Mexico since 1994 under the North American Free Trade Agreement (NAFTA). But the results of the CAFTA negotiations could offset some of the benefits obtained by the Dominican Republic under the CBTPA.

Although close to half of the FTZ exports are still in textiles, especially assembly of clothing, in 2000 there were electronics exports worth US\$570 million, US\$460 million from exports of jewellery, US\$320 million from sales of medical products, and US$330 million from tobacco products such as cigars. Data also shows that more value is now being added to these exports within the Dominican Republic.

In February 2003, President Mejía announced that he had enlisted a new partner, *Dubai's Ports, Customs and Free Zone Corporation*, in a scheme to develop a port and free trade zone on the coast of Monte Cristi, in the north-western corner of the country, in what may become the largest single foreign investment in the Dominican Republic (US$4.1 billion). The Dubai firm has signed a 19-year concession to develop and manage a 30-square-kilometre FTZ, a port complex, a cargo airport and a passenger airport near the city of Monte Cristi. The proposed project will be developed in an area the size of a medium-sized city. It includes the modernization of the current port of Manzanillo, the construction of a container ship and cargo freight facility, 1 000 hotel rooms, a 400-ship full service marina, an industrial FTZ, an ecological park, an airport, urban development projects, potable water and sewage infrastructure, a 100-megawatt power plant, a waste recycling facility, and highways. In 2001 it had been announced that *Trans Dominicana de Desarrollo* (a consortium comprising Groupe Balguerie of France, Nesebe-Emirat of the United Arab Emirates, and US operators Royal Caribbean Cruises and Carnival) would make a US$1.4-billion investment over a seven-year period in the north-western provinces of Monte Cristi and Dajabon. Groupe Balguerie of France has been placed in charge of the port development, in conjunction with the shipping companies Maersk, Evergreen and CMA-CGM. The airport will be the investment of the Groupe Egis of France. Carnival, Four Seasons and Accor tourism companies will develop the tourism ventures.

## 1.6. Economic impact of FDI and linkages with the local economy

It is estimated that there are 350 000 jobs that are directly the result of FDI. There is no data on the impact of FDI on indirect jobs but it could be extrapolated that it is at least of the same order of magnitude as the direct impact. In the FTZ sector, women account for 55.2 per cent of all jobs. The average salary paid by foreign affiliates is US$286.50 monthly (which is also the country's average salary), whereas the country's legal minimum salary is of US$142 monthly.

One key component of the FDI linkages with local companies and workers is the on-the-job training received by Dominican employees working for foreign firms. There is considerable evidence, in the case of the Dominican Republic, that unskilled workers are able to reach between 60 and 80 per cent of best-practice labor productivity in the home countries of the investors.[8] Efforts should be devoted to increase this percentage to 100 per cent in order to ensure that Dominican workers can match the skills of those in investors'

Table 1.8. **FDI inflows as a percentage of GDP and gross fixed capital formation 1995-2000**

Million of US dollars and percentage

|  | 1995 | 1996 | 1997 | 1998 | 1999 | 2000 |
|---|---|---|---|---|---|---|
| FDI | 414.3 | 96.5 | 420.6 | 699.8 | 1 337.8 | 952.9 |
| GDP | 11 994.3 | 13 335.4 | 15 081.5 | 15 873.2 | 17 363.5 | 19 711.0 |
| Gross fixed capital formation | 2 238.9 | 2 533.7 | 2 986.1 | 3 714.3 | 4 261.9 | 4 671.5 |
| FDI/GDP (%) | 3.5 | 0.7 | 2.8 | 4.4 | 7.7 | 4.8 |
| FDI/gross fixed capital formation (%) | 18.5 | 3.8 | 14.1 | 18.8 | 31.4 | 20.4 |

1. Preliminary data.

Source: International Department, Central Bank of the Dominican Republic.

home countries. In the Dominican Republic as well as in several other countries, evidence shows that spillovers to the local economy is the strongest when there is educational training.

Another winning strategy adopted by the Dominican Republic with respect to linkages with the local economy was to create FTZs near industrial and commercial centres, thereby allowing foreign investors to be near skilled labor, who is then able to benefit from spillover effects. But more remains to be done. To reap the full benefits of FTZs, it is essential to have better infrastructure and overall trade and investment liberalization providing a level-playing field to local companies so that they can compete to sell inputs to FTZ firms.

## 1.7. Future perspectives

The foreign investment regime should be not adversely affected by any change at the political helm of the country when the presidential elections take place in May 2004 since all three main political parties share essentially the same views on the need to attract FDI. On May 16, 2002, the country's legislative and municipal elections gave the ruling *Partido Revolucionario Dominicano* (Dominican Revolutionary Party) (PRD) of President Hipólito Mejía nearly the entire senate but the PRD does not have an absolute majority in the lower house as it did before the elections. The PRD captured 73 seats; the *Partido de la Liberación Dominicana* (Dominican Liberation Party) (PLD), 41; and the *Partido Reformista Social Cristiano* (Christian Social Reform Party) (PRSC), 36.

ISBN 92-64-10509-3
OECD Investment Policy Reviews
Caribbean Rim: Costa Rica, Dominican Republic and Jamaica
© OECD 2004

# *Chapter 2*

# Investment Environment

## 2.1. Structure of the economy

The Dominican Republic's GDP grew from US$13.56 billion in 1996 to US$19.81 billion in 2000. The growth in the Dominican economy in the second half of the 1990s is the result of private sector consumption and investment, and growth in exports. In 2000, for example, private consumption accounted for 77.5 per cent of GDP, whereas the private investment's contribution was of 19.4 per cent. In contrast, government consumption had a small share of 8.2 per cent and public investment had a smaller share of 4.4 per cent. Exports of goods and services at 45.5 per cent of GDP in 2000 and imports of goods and services at 55 per cent are the other two key components of the gross domestic product.

As mentioned above, during the second half of the 1990s, the Dominican Republic enjoyed strong economic growth with an average annual rate of 7.7 per cent, becoming the fastest growing Latin American and Caribbean economy. Communications at an average rate of 17.4 per cent per year led the other sectors. Construction came second at 14.5 per cent. Tourism also exhibited very high growth with an average annual rate of 11.8 per cent, and so did the electricity, gas, and water sector at 10.7 per cent.

Other sectors also made significant contribution to GDP growth during the period from 1996 and 2000. Wholesale and retail trade contributed 15.2 per cent to GDP growth and transportation 8.1 per cent. Both sectors grew at an average annual rate of 9.2 per cent. FTZs suffered after the implementation of the NAFTA. Facing trade diversion particularly due to the stringent NAFTA rules of origin in textiles and apparel, FTZs grew at a more modest average annual rate of 4.5 per cent during the second half of the 1990s. As noted in Section 1.5.3 on efficiency-seeking FDI, this sector stands to gain from the CBTPA, which provides a level-playing field with the NAFTA. Traditional manufacturing, in contrast, grew at a faster average annual rate of 6.8 per cent as a result of the modernization of old industrial infrastructure.

As a whole, the services sector contributed to 54.9 per cent of the country's GDP growth between 1996 and 2000. As the Dominican Republic becomes more dependent on services and manufacturing, the share of agriculture in the gross domestic product has been declining steadily for the past 20 years, from 20.1 per cent in 1980 to 11.1 per cent in 2000, as seen in Table 2.1.

Table 2.1. **Main economic sectors as a percentage of GDP selected years**

% of GDP

|  | 1980 | 1990 | 1999 | 2000 |
|---|---|---|---|---|
| Agriculture | 20.1 | 13.4 | 11.4 | 11.1 |
| Industry | 28.3 | 31.4 | 34.2 | 34.1 |
| Manufacturing | 15.3 | 18.0 | 16.8 | 17.0 |
| Services | 51.6 | 55.2 | 54.5 | 54.8 |
| Private consumption | 77.0 | 79.6 | 75.2 | 77.7 |
| General government consumption | 7.6 | 5.1 | 8.1 | 8.2 |

Source: Central Bank of the Dominican Republic.

A more in-depth analysis of the Dominican economy shows that the agriculture, livestock, fishing, and forestry sector is dominated by small domestic producers. Although this sector has experienced an average annual growth of 5 per cent between 1996 and 2000, its share of total GDP has decreased due to faster growth rates in other sectors. Exports of agricultural goods were severely affected by the damage caused by Hurricane Georges in 1998. Total exports of primary agricultural products accounted for 7.3 per cent of GDP in 1996 and only 2.3 per cent in 2000. The Government has traditionally been very involved in the agricultural sector but in recent years it has limited its intervention to price-stabilization arrangements and financial help for small producers through the *Banco Agrícola de la República Dominicana*.

The other key component of primary production is mining, which is concentrated in nickel-iron, marble and quarry products. The mining sector experienced a major decline in 1998 (15.9 per cent) when nickel prices fell sharply. A smaller contraction (1.5 per cent) in 1999 was followed by strong growth (9.2 per cent) in 2000. Production of *doré* (an alloy of gold and silver) ceased in 1999 when Rosario Dominicana, then owned by the Central Bank, faced financial and technical problems. In July 2001, the concession of Pueblo Viejo, where the sulphide deposits are located, was awarded to Canadian-based Placer Dome, subject to ratification by Congress.

The traditional manufacturing sector, which consists of flour, vegetable oils, fertilisers, cement, sugar, alcoholic beverage such as beer, rum and whiskey, steel bars, pharmaceutical products, and plastic derivatives, grew substantially during the second half of the 1990s, with an average annual growth of 6.8 per cent. It benefited from increased investment in infrastructure as a result of tariff reform implemented in 1990, stronger domestic demand, and liberalization of foreign direct investment.

The FTZ sector is made of industrial parks, located throughout the country, whose vocation is to manufacture products for export. As firms which settled in the FTZs do not pay import duties, they operate in their own free trade area. Their contribution to GDP growth has been a steady 3.2 per cent per year, whereas their contribution to exports and foreign exchange earnings has been spectacular. FTZs account for 83.2 per cent of all Dominican exports (see Annex 1). They were the second largest source of foreign currency in the Dominican Republic between 1996 and 2000 with US$1.71 billion, ahead of workers' remittances (US$1.69 billion) but behind tourism (US$2.86 billion). More than 200 000 Dominicans have found employment in FTZs. While investors who need a more sophisticated labor force have opted to locate near the capital, there are FTZs located throughout the country. In addition to the traditional textile and apparel manufacturing, other products are now manufactured in the free trade zones. Electronics, jewellery, medical products, metal products, and data processing are among the new FTZ sectors.

Table 2.2. **Gross domestic product by sector**

As a percentage of GDP, at constant 1970 prices

| | 1996 | 1997 | 1998 | 1999 | 2000 |
|---|---|---|---|---|---|
| **Primary production** | | | | | |
| Agriculture, livestock, fishing and forestry | 12.8 | 12.2 | 11.5 | 11.4 | 11.1 |
| Mining | 2.6 | 2.5 | 2.0 | 1.8 | 1.8 |
| Total primary production | 15.5 | 14.7 | 13.5 | 13.2 | 12.9 |
| **Secondary production** | | | | | |
| Manufacturing | | | | | |
| Traditional | 14.0 | 13.8 | 13.5 | 13.6 | 13.8 |
| FTZs | 3.5 | 3.5 | 3.5 | 3.2 | 3.2 |
| Total manufacturing | 17.5 | 17.3 | 17.1 | 16.8 | 17.0 |
| Electricity, gas, and water[1] | 2.0 | 2.0 | 2.1 | 2.1 | 2.2 |
| Construction | 10.2 | 11.0 | 12.3 | 13.4 | 13.1 |
| Total secondary production | 29.7 | 30.4 | 31.5 | 32.4 | 32.3 |
| **Services** | | | | | |
| Wholesale and retail trade | 12.3 | 12.5 | 12.9 | 13.0 | 13.0 |
| Hotels, bars and restaurants | 6.0 | 6.5 | 6.3 | 6.4 | 6.8 |
| Transportation | 6.8 | 6.9 | 7.0 | 6.9 | 7.2 |
| Communications | 3.8 | 4.2 | 4.7 | 5.0 | 5.4 |
| Financial services | 4.7 | 4.4 | 4.3 | 4.2 | 4.0 |
| Real estate | 5.0 | 4.7 | 4.5 | 4.2 | 4.0 |
| Public administration | 8.4 | 8.0 | 7.8 | 7.5 | 7.2 |
| Other | 8.1 | 7.8 | 7.6 | 7.3 | 7.1 |
| Total services | 54.9 | 54.9 | 55.0 | 54.4 | 54.8 |
| **Total GDP** | **100.0** | **100.0** | **100.0** | **100.0** | **100.0** |

1. Although listed here in secondary production, electricity, gas and water could also have been included under services, as noted in other parts of this document.

Source: Central Bank of the Dominican Republic.

Electricity, gas and water are sectors in expansion, and so is the construction sector which benefited from construction of hotels, highways, dams, bridges, shopping centres, houses and office buildings in recent years.

The services sector in the Dominican Republic continues to be very dynamic. Multinational corporations have now entered the wholesale and retail trade sector, particularly through the large supermarkets, the fast-food business, the clothing stores, and franchising. Hotels, bars and restaurants have greatly benefited from the growth in tourism. Transportation has also grown rapidly in recent years, as a result of the modernization of the country's infrastructure.

The 1990s witnessed the arrival of competition in the telecommunication sector, first with the launch in 1992 of TRICOM as a provider of telephone service, and in 2000 when France Telecom and Centennial Dominicana (a subsidiary of Centennial Communication Corporation) entered the wireless and fixed line telephone markets. As emphasized above, the communication sector registered the highest growth rate in the Dominican economy during the second half of the 1990s. The financial sector, in contrast, grew at a much lower rate, i.e. an average annual growth rate of 3.3 per cent, which explains why the sector accounts for a smaller share of GDP in 2000 (4 per cent) than in 1996 (4.7 per cent). The Mejía Government has promised to pursue the opening up of the financial services sector to foreign investment.

On the macroeconomic front, the country has also been performing very well, albeit the situation worsened in 2002 and at the beginning of 2003. With respect to public sector external debt, the Dominican Republic is the Latin American and Caribbean country with the best grade report. Public sector debt declined significantly during the 1990s, from 28.1 per cent of GDP and 60.6 per cent of total exports of goods and services in 1996 to 18.6 per cent of GDP and 41 per cent of total exports in 2000 (Table 2.3). These percentages are very low when compared to other countries in the region, as shown in Table 2.4. Also worth emphasizing is that the external debt service to GDP ratio as well as the external debt service to total exports ratio are also low.

Table 2.3. **Public external debt and external debt service**

| | 1996 | 1997 | 1998 | 1999 | 2000 |
|---|---|---|---|---|---|
| Public sector external debt as a percentage of GDP | 28.1 | 23.5 | 22.2 | 20.9 | 18.6 |
| Public sector external debt as a percentage of total exports | 60.6 | 53.1 | 47.4 | 45.8 | 41.0 |
| External debt service as a percentage of GDP | 3.1 | 2.5 | 2.5 | 2.3 | 2.9 |
| External debt service as a percentage of total exports | 6.6 | 5.5 | 5.5 | 5.1 | 6.3 |
| External debt service as a percentage of total exports and workers' remittances | 5.8 | 4.7 | 4.6 | 4.3 | 5.4 |
| External debt service as a percentage of total fiscal revenue | 21.7 | 15.7 | 16.0 | 14.7 | 18.0 |

Source: IMF and Central Bank of the Dominican Republic.

Table 2.4. **External debt to GDP and total exports ratios for various Latin American and Caribbean countries**

| | External debt as a percentage of GDP (2000) | External debt as a percentage of total exports (2000) |
|---|---|---|
| Argentina | 62.0 | 484.7 |
| Jamaica | 61.4 | 85.7 |
| Panama | 58.0 | 122.6 |
| Colombia | 42.3 | 202.3 |
| Brazil | 40.5 | 340.0 |
| Costa Rica | 35.9 | 44.3 |
| Mexico | 32.2 | 92.6 |
| El Salvador | 27.0 | 78.2 |
| **Dominican Republic** | **18.6** | **41.0** |

Source: Moody's Investor Service.

The current account deficit as a percentage of GDP decreased in 2001 to 3.6 per cent but increased in 2002 to 3.8 per cent. The trade deficit on goods and services was financed by continued remittances from the one million Dominicans leaving abroad. FDI inflows will help finance the current account deficit in 2003 but an increase in external net indebtedness is also possible. Also worth noting is that the peso lost of one third of its value in 2002, despite monetary tightening and heavy intervention on the foreign exchange market by the Central Bank.

Table 2.5. **Current account deficit in absolute terms and relative to GDP and FDI 1995-2000**

Million of US dollars and percentage

| | 1995 | 1996 | 1997 | 1998 | 1999 | 2000[1] |
|---|---|---|---|---|---|---|
| Current account deficit | 182.8 | 212.7 | 167 | 338.2 | 429.1 | 1 026.5 |
| GDP | 11 994.3 | 13 335.4 | 15 081.5 | 15 873.2 | 17 363.5 | 19 711.0 |
| Current account deficit/GDP (%) | 1.5 | 1.6 | 1.1 | 2.1 | 2.5 | 5.2 |
| Current account deficit/FDI (%) | 44.12 | 220.41 | 39.71 | 48.33 | 32.08 | 107.71 |

1. Preliminary data.
Source: International Department, Central Bank of the Dominican Republic.

## 2.2. Infrastructure

Transport, communications, and electricity are the key components of the country's infrastructure. While transport services accounted for 6.6 per cent of the Dominican GDP in 2001, communications amounted to 6.5 per cent during the same year. Improvement of the infrastructure in both sectors is a top priority of the Government.

OECD INVESTMENT POLICY REVIEWS – ISBN 92-64-10509-3 – © OECD 2004

## Road and maritime transport

The Dominican Republic has a total of 12 600 kilometres of roads, including 6 200 of which are paved. Non-electrified railway consists of 757 kilometres, of which 240 are run by sugar companies. In February 2003, President Mejía announced the construction of the San Pedro de Macoris-La Romana highway expansion. The Government has entrusted the Spanish-Dominican engineering firm *Concesionaria Dominicana de Autopistas y Carreteras* with the 30-year concession contract. Construction time is estimated to take two years. The Government will install 10 new toll stations to increase collections to pay for the new highway improvements. Additionally, the Government plans to begin expansion of the La Romana-Higuey and Higuey-Veron (Punta Cana) highway this year.

The country is also home to eleven – state-owned – maritime ports, whereas the private sector is an active participant in the construction of a multi-modal port.[9] The construction work at the Multimodal Terminal at Punta Caucedo has advanced significantly, with partial operation of the country's first terminal of mega-ship capacity expected to begin by the end of 2003. The 50-hectare Caucedo Terminal will provide extensive container handling capability to and from the Dominican Republic. The port's location in the centre of North-South and East-West trade lanes is expected to competitively position the Caucedo port as a transhipment hub of the Caribbean. The country will also greatly benefit from lower freight rates. Currently, the cost of shipping a container from Santo Domingo to Miami is US$2 800, from Costa Rica to Miami it is US$2 000 and from Honduras, it amounts to US$1 800.[10]

A new international tourist docking facility opened in the Port of La Romana in December 2002. About US$12 million dollars were invested in the new wharfs and an estimated 147 000 vacationers, travelling on 67 cruise ships, are expected to use this facility during the 2002-2003 year.

It takes five to ten hours for a good to clear customs. On average, it will take the Dominican from one day to one and a half day to take possession of his good. There is a system that allows the company to pay the necessary charges before the shipment arrives at port. With respect to exported goods, it may take up to five days (goods to the United States) or as little as one day and half (Puerto Rico) for a shipment to reach the premises of the importer after the ship has docked in the port. Fees and charges (other than duties and applicable taxes) imposed on or in connection with imports are the commission of 4.75 per cent on foreign-exchange transactions; the fee to Hispaniola Dispatch, which fluctuates depending on the time the ship is docked in the port, the storage fee calculated per week with a minimum of $400 Dominican pesos a week for a minimum of 1 000 kilos. If the shipment is in transit, the importer only pays for the time the ship stays in the port, which is an average of $0.45 cents for each 100 kilos stored.

## Air transport

The Dominican Republic has ten major airports. The airports of Santo Domingo (Las Americas), Punta Cana, La Romana and Puerto Plata are served by national airlines, numerous charters, and major international airlines. As a result of the Government's privatization policy, six airports were granted in concession to Aerodom, an international consortium, for 25 years until 2024. The concession requires Aerodom to expand and renovate airport facilities.

Air transport is governed by the Civil Aviation Law (Law No. 505) of November 10, 1969, and Law No. 8 of November 19, 1978, establishing the Airport Commission to manage all Dominican airports. While national air transport is reserved for companies that are owned by natural Dominicans, international air transport is subject to concession. Open skies agreements with Chile, Central American countries, and the United States (signed but not ratified) have also been concluded.

## Telecommunications

With respect to the communication system, it is worth noting that the Government has launched a number of initiatives aimed at enhancing that system. For instance, it is allocating 60 per cent of a 2 per cent excise tax on communication services to improve access to telephone and other communication services. The level of penetration of phone service keeps increasing in the country, from 9 telephone lines for every 100 residents in 1996 to 18.7 telephone lines for every 100 residents by the end of 2000. It takes 10 to 20 days for a line to be granted and installed. Moreover, fixed wire and cellular phones had reached 2.225 million by the end of 2001. Internet access also increased in recent years, by an average of 75 per cent.

The telecommunications sectors is regulated by the Telecommunications Law[11] and regulations issued by INDOTEL, the Dominican Institute of Telecommunications. INDOTEL promotes investment in the sector and supervises service providers who are free to set rates for telecommunications services, albeit INDOTEL can intervene if it estimates that market conditions do not ensure competition.

## Electricity

The surge in electricity demand fuelled by the strong growth in the Dominican economy has not been met by a similar increase in generating capacity despite the record level in FDI in that sector. In fact, insufficient investment in generating capacity and an overburdened transmission and distribution system have resulted in blackouts. To avoid suffering from the effects of these blackouts which are less frequent but still occurring, several companies have opted to install their own power generation, to ensure reliable electricity supplies. It is worth noting that despite existing problems, private firms have been investing heavily in the country's electricity infrastructure.[12]

## 2.3. Human capital

The Dominican labor force is large, young, and very urban. Labor laws do not prohibit strikes or the establishment of trade unions, and the labor code expressly indicates that 80 per cent of the employees in each firm must be Dominican.

In recent years, GDP growth has had a positive impact on the unemployment rate in the country, as it fell from 16.7 per cent in 1996 to 13.9 per cent in 2000. The key sectors in terms of employment are wholesale and retail trade, construction, manufacturing and agriculture, as show in Table 2.6.

Table 2.6. **Employment**
Percentage by sector

|  | 1996 | 1997 | 1998 | 1999 | 2000 |
|---|---|---|---|---|---|
| Agriculture, livestock, fishing and forestry | 19.9 | 20.0 | 17.1 | 17.5 | 16.3 |
| Mining | 0.4 | 0.3 | 0.3 | 0.3 | 0.2 |
| Manufacturing | 18.5 | 17.9 | 18.4 | 17.4 | 17.0 |
| Construction | 6.7 | 6.8 | 6.9 | 7.2 | 6.3 |
| Electricity, gas and water | 0.5 | 0.5 | 0.5 | 0.4 | 0.8 |
| Transportation and communications | 6.7 | 7.0 | 6.9 | 7.3 | 6.2 |
| Wholesale and retail trade | 19.8 | 20.0 | 21.7 | 21.9 | 21.7 |
| Financial services | 1.4 | 1.3 | 1.3 | 1.3 | 1.9 |
| Public administration and defense | 4.0 | 3.8 | 3.6 | 3.6 | 4.2 |
| Hotels, bars and restaurants | 4.8 | 4.8 | 4.8 | 4.8 | 5.2 |
| Other services | 17.5 | 17.6 | 18.3 | 18.3 | 20.4 |
| Total | 100.0 | 100.0 | 100.0 | 100.0 | 100.0 |

Source: Central Bank.

Low-skilled labor is available and the Dominican workforce is known for being highly "competent, trainable, and cooperative", but skilled workers are a scarce resource. When international competitiveness depends on labor costs, the Dominican Republic is more competitive than Costa Rica and Jamaica. However, hourly-wage rates are higher in the Dominican Republic than in Guatemala and Mexico, without an equivalent increase in labor productivity.

Investment in education, which currently represents only 2.5 per cent of GDP, would contribute greatly to increase the supply of technically skilled labor, and help enhance the Dominican Republic's efforts to attract foreign investment. Measures to better train workers would also have long lasting benefit for the domestic economy. Well-targeted training programs could serve to improve prospects for employment and raise the productivity of workers so as to meet the needs of businesses.

The education system consists of public and private schools which offer pre-school, primary and secondary education. Approximately 85 per cent of Dominican children aged 6 to 13 are enrolled in primary school. The level for secondary school is 65 per cent.

The country is home to one public university, the *Universidad Autónoma de Santo Domingo*, founded in 1538 and the oldest university in the Americas, numerous (more than 30) private universities, as well as seven institutes of higher education. The average tuition fee for an undergraduate degree is of US$300, whereas the average cost to obtain a diploma from an institution of higher education is approximately US$3 600.

The adult literacy rate is 84.5 per cent, whereas it is 86 per cent in Jamaica and 91 per cent in Colombia, Mexico and Panama, and 95 per cent in Costa Rica.

## 2.4. Public governance: transparency, integrity, and rule of law

Many sectors of the Dominican economy – mostly export-oriented industries – have enjoyed a high degree of transparency in their relationship with government agencies. While in those cases red tape is almost non existent and the use of permits and paperwork minimal, progress is being made to ensure that the other sectors of the economy share the same benefits. One key element of the Mejía program is to end the so-called *grado a grado* (step by step) system, whereby Government contracts may be awarded without recourse to a competitive bidding process. This system is widely held to be the major source of public corruption. The government procurement system of the country is currently under review. A new law adopted in February 2001 (Law No. 27-01) prohibits the Government from buying imported goods and services, should a national product exists. Government procurement is also regulated by Law No. 295 of June 30, 1966 and a decree adopted in 1998. Essentially, these laws and regulations stipulate that purchases by public enterprises are not covered and that public bidding must take place, provided that preference is given to domestic suppliers. For purchases below RD$ 100 000, five offers should be invited. For purchases above RD$ 100 000 but below RD$ 3 million, at least ten enterprises must be invited to bid. Finally, direct contracting is used for smaller purchases.

For the first time in 2001, the Dominican Republic was included in the Corruption Perceptions Index of Transparency International. The country ranked 63rd out of 91 countries in 2001 and improved its score in 2002 ranking 59th out of 102 countries, ahead of Guatemala, Venezuela, Honduras, Nicaragua, Ecuador, and Bolivia but behind Chile, Trinidad and Tobago, Uruguay, Costa Rica, Colombia and Mexico (Table 2.7).

Table 2.7. **Corruption perceptions index for Latin American and Caribbean countries**

|  | Rank in 2001 | Rank in 2002 |
|---|---|---|
| Chile | 18 | 17 |
| Uruguay | 35 | 32 |
| Trinidad and Tobago | 32 | 33 |
| Costa Rica | 40 | 40 |
| Peru | 44 | 45 |
| Brazil | 46 | 45 |
| Colombia | 50 | 57 |
| Mexico | 51 | 57 |
| **Dominican Republic** | **63** | **59** |
| El Salvador | 55 | 62 |
| Panama | 52 | 67 |
| Argentina | 57 | 70 |
| Honduras | 71 | 71 |
| Guatemala | 65 | 81 |
| Venezuela | 70 | 81 |
| Nicaragua | 78 | 81 |
| Ecuador | 79 | 89 |
| Bolivia | 85 | 89 |

*Source:* Transparency International (*www.transparency.org*).

Article 102 of the Constitution provides for the sanction of acts of corruption. The Penal, Labor and Tributary Codes and the laws and regulations of the Secretaries of State (State Ministries) punish the acts of corruption. There have been twelve well-known cases involving high Government officials charged with corruption; seven belong to the past Government administration and five to the current administration. All are still pending in courts.

It is worth emphasizing that since January 1, 2003, a person applying for a public sector job under the Civil Services and Administrative Career Law is required to compete for posts based on his/her merits and work experience. This measure will undoubtedly contribute to reducing corruption and favoritism in the public sector.

In February 2003, President Mejia also announced that he was sending bills to Congress aimed at fighting against government corruption. One of the bills would transfer the power to appoint the national controller to the Senate, instead of the Executive Branch. When introducing the proposal, the President said the intent was to make the position of controller independent from the Executive Branch. President Mejia also tabled a bill that would create a department – *Fiscalia Anticorrupción* – to fight corruption. A third project would oblige officers to indicate the source of any increased wealth after their term in government. Finally, the President announced that he would resubmit another bill to Congress, which would guarantee the press free access to government information. The *Ley de Acceso a la Información Pública* would oblige Government officials to reveal information they commonly refuse to make public today.

The Dominican Republic does not have a competition policy law, albeit legislation on consumer protection and competition was tabled before Congress in 1998, but not adopted. A new draft law is in the making. Competition provisions are contained in the Constitution, the Penal Code, the Copyright Law, and the Industrial Property Law. For instance, Article 8 of the Constitution protects the exercise of free enterprise and prohibits monopolies of private corporations; albeit it allows state monopolies and those provided for by law. The Penal Code prohibits collusion among business executives, particularly with respect to price setting. Moreover, Law No. 13 of April 1963 permits price controls for certain basic articles and services with a view to protecting consumers, whereas Law No. 112-00 of November 2000 allows the Ministry of Industry and Trade to determine retail prices for petroleum and petroleum products on a weekly basis.[13]

It takes on average 45 to 60 days for an administrative dispute settlement procedure to reach a final decision regarding a particular measure. However, the parties could ask for ten days in each instance to deposit documents, which can postpone the process for 30 additional days.

All laws regulating sectors of the economy establish deadlines or specific timeframes to grant permits and licenses. In practice, however, they are rarely observed, but the silence of management should not be understood as implicit authorization. The *litigious administrative* procedure mandates conciliation before a claim can be brought but it does not contemplate any type of arbitration. If all three instances are pursued it can take from three to five years for an administrative dispute to be adjudicated in domestic courts.

The Constitution does not establish that international obligations have a higher status that domestic legislation. An international treaty needs to be ratified by Congress in order to be implemented in the country. The Constitution does not establish that private parties can invoke international agreement as applicable law in domestic courts but when international agreements enter into force, they acquire force of law and can be used/argued in national courts just as the domestic legislation.

## 2.5. Trade regime

In recent years, the Dominican Republic has moved forward and liberalized its trade regime, becoming one of the most open economies in Latin America, as a result of relatively low effective average import tariffs and the establishment of free trade zones. In fact, trade played a significant role in

**42**

the increase in the gross domestic product (GDP) during the 1990s. As Table 2.8 shows, exports accounted for approximately 30 per cent of annual GDP growth with the notable exception of 1992. Moreover, the high level of openness of the Dominican economy is reflected in high imports and exports of goods and services to GDP ratio, which reached 100.5 per cent in 2000.

Table 2.8. **Export to GDP ratio**
Million of US dollars and percentage

|  | Exports | GDP | Exports/GDP |
|---|---|---|---|
| 1990 | 1 584.7 | 5 537.7 | 28.6 |
| 1991 | 1 711.2 | 7 479.3 | 22.9 |
| 1992 | 1 757.7 | 8 901.9 | 19.7 |
| 1993 | 3 211.0 | 9 690.4 | 33.1 |
| 1994 | 3 452.5 | 10 697.2 | 32.3 |
| 1995 | 3 779.5 | 11 994.3 | 31.5 |
| 1996 | 4 052.8 | 13 335.4 | 30.4 |
| 1997 | 4 613.8 | 15 081.5 | 30.6 |
| 1998 | 4 980.5 | 15 873.2 | 31.4 |
| 1999 | 5 136.7 | 17 363.5 | 29.6 |
| 2000 | 5 736.7 | 19 711.0 | 29.1 |

Source: Central Bank of the Dominican Republic.

As shown in Table 2.9, the United States is the single most important export market for Dominican products. In 2000, 72 per cent of all exports from the Dominican Republic were destined to the United States. Puerto Rico came second with 15.5 per cent of all Dominican exports, whereas neighboring Haiti accounted for 2 per cent. North America's (including Mexico) share totalled 88 per cent, whereas Latin America and the Caribbean's (excluding Mexico) share was of 4.2 per cent, Europe's 6.2 per cent, Asia's 1.3 per cent, and Africa's 0.1 per cent.

As exports from FTZs represent the bulk of all Dominican exports, accounting for 83.2 per cent of total exports in 2000 (see Annex 1), in practice, as noted by the WTO in its Trade Policy Review of the Dominican Republic published in September 2002, "most of the Dominican Republic's merchandise trade is not governed by the rules of its general trade regime. This reflects the recognition that the [general] regime still creates an anti-export bias despite continuing liberalization, and the desire to assist exports by offering exporters special rules, notably under the free-trade zone regime".[14] Further trade liberalization is therefore needed, albeit the tariff reform approved in December 2000 cut the maximum import tariff from 35 per cent to 20 per cent, and the number of tariffs from nine (35 per cent, 30 per cent, 25 per cent, 20 per cent, 15 per cent, 10 per cent, 5 per cent, 1.5 per cent, and 0 per cent) to

Table 2.9. **Exports by country of destination, 1997-2000**
Thousands of US dollars

|  | 1997 | 1998 | 1999 | 2000[1] |
|---|---|---|---|---|
| United States | 3 089 232 | 3 391 232 | 3 704 447 | 4 116 836 |
| Puerto Rico | 888 658 | 946 448 | 843 514 | 886 902 |
| Haití | 35 995 | 35 441 | 67 860 | 114 114 |
| Belgium | 133 539 | 102 733 | 106 222 | 99 905 |
| The Netherlands | 30 588 | 44 314 | 50 989 | 63 188 |
| United Kingdom | 59 069 | 102 259 | 38 306 | 41 272 |
| Canada | 36 224 | 41 875 | 46 399 | 40 865 |
| Germany | 19 957 | 27 914 | 22 870 | 37 214 |
| France | 16 414 | 21 504 | 17 898 | 35 329 |
| Korea | 51 436 | 27 480 | 34 355 | 27 691 |
| Italy | 28 924 | 27 150 | 19 374 | 27 246 |
| Spain | 18 927 | 18 463 | 15 201 | 23 314 |
| Honduras | 23 042 | 17 049 | 12 852 | 19 571 |
| Japan | 28 166 | 19 807 | 12 434 | 11 738 |
| Jamaica | 16 049 | 17 309 | 9 601 | 11 461 |

1. Preliminary data.
Source: Central Bank of the Dominican Republic; International Department; Balance of Payments Sub-Direction; Export and Import Analysis Division.

five (20 per cent, 14 per cent, 8 per cent, 3 per cent, and 0 per cent). The 2000 tariff reform was the second to be implemented by the country in recent years. In 1990, the Dominican Republic had reduced its maximum tariff to 35 per cent from a tariff exceeding 200 per cent.

The current import tariff structure is as follows:

a) 20 per cent tariff applies to most consumer goods;

b) 14 per cent tariff applies to certain intermediate goods;

c) 8 per cent tariff applies primarily to raw materials and capital goods;

d) 3 per cent tariff applies primarily to supplies, machinery and equipment used in the textile, agricultural and livestock sectors, and education materials.

In 2000, the effective average import tariff was of 16.9 per cent.

In February 2003, the Government imposed by decree a 10 per cent surcharge on all imports – except food, medicines, raw materials and capital goods – for a period of 90 days, as part of a series of measures to promote austerity in an attempt to curb the depreciation of the exchange rate.

Textiles at 43.5 per cent, electronics at 9.9 per cent, and jewellery at 8 per cent are the key components of FTZ exports. Traditional exports (sugar and related products, coffee, cocoa, tobacco, and nickel-iron) represented only 7.5 per cent of all Dominican exports in 2000. Non-traditional exports such as

OECD INVESTMENT POLICY REVIEWS – ISBN 92-64-10509-3 – © OECD 2004

beer and fruits have been growing over the past few years. In 2000, they accounted for 6.1 per cent of total exports.

The dependency of the Dominican Republic on the North American market is not as pronounced in the case of imports. In 2000, North America accounted for 65.7 per cent of all Dominican imports, whereas Latin America and the Caribbean's share reached 16.9 per cent, Europe's 8.7 per cent, and Asia's 8.3 per cent. As shown in Table 2.10, the five most important trading partners on the import side were the United States (52.5 per cent), Venezuela (10.4 per cent), Puerto Rico (7.9 per cent), Mexico (4.7 per cent) and Japan (3 per cent). Spain – the largest foreign investor in the country during the second half of the 1990s – ranked sixth with 2.7 per cent of all Dominican imports, and captured only 0.4 per cent of all Dominican exports.

Table 2.10. **Imports by country of origin, 1997-2000**
Thousands of US dollars

|  | 1997 | 1998 | 1999 | 2000 |
|---|---|---|---|---|
| United States | 3 779 567 | 4 251 469 | 4 148 521 | 4 981 228 |
| Venezuela | 507 518 | 443 093 | 671 060 | 981 269 |
| Puerto Rico | 509 550 | 706 515 | 1 094 685 | 752 431 |
| Mexico | 312 497 | 300 084 | 265 331 | 447 974 |
| Japan | 191 910 | 219 609 | 240 907 | 280 857 |
| Spain | 98 877 | 175 694 | 217 390 | 252 844 |
| Panama | 119 901 | 111 959 | 122 323 | 160 798 |
| Germany | 57 847 | 81 365 | 122 245 | 151 985 |
| South Korea | 47 839 | 110 790 | 178 119 | 149 678 |
| Taiwan | 78 559 | 112 037 | 88 316 | 124 426 |
| Brazil | 48 184 | 83 069 | 82 790 | 96 262 |
| Italy | 51 733 | 74 587 | 47 936 | 82 828 |
| Colombia | 64 243 | 64 064 | 68 634 | 77 609 |
| France | 44 802 | 28 494 | 32 819 | 64 289 |
| Denmark | 54 230 | 52 742 | 41 267 | 48 809 |

Note: Countries of destination and origin are determined on the basis of declarations made by each importer to the General Customs Administration.
1. Preliminary data.
Source: Central Bank of the Dominican Republic; International Department; Balance of Payments Sub-Direction; Export and Import Analysis Division.

Although the import share of FTZs has slightly fallen in relative terms during the second part of the 1990s, it remains fairly significant representing 32.3 per cent of all imports into the Dominican Republic in 2000 (see Annex 2).

The services sector is also a key element of the Dominican Republic's foreign trade. Tourism is the single most important component of the country's services trade. In 2000, income from tourism reached US$2.9 billion.

The Dominican Republic joined the General Agreement on Tariffs and Trade (GATT) in 1950 and has been a member of the World Trade Organization since its inception. It has also been an active participant in the Free Trade Area of the Americas (FTAA) process since 1994. In addition, the country is participating in a number of other trade initiatives. In April 1998, it signed a free trade agreement with the members of the Central American Common Market (Costa Rica, El Salvador, Guatemala, Honduras, and Nicaragua). In August 1998, a trade agreement was signed with CARICOM members. Moreover, since 1983, the Dominican Republic has been one of the twenty-four beneficiaries of the Caribbean Basin Initiative, which was enhanced by the Caribbean Basin Trade Partnership Act. Exports under both programs reached US$2.4 billion in 2001. The country has also been party to the Cotonou Agreement, formerly known as the Lomé Convention, under which the European Union offers economic cooperation and assistance to partner countries in Africa, the Caribbean and the Pacific. Dominican agricultural goods, textiles and electronic components are granted preferential access under that agreement. Moreover, the Dominican Republic benefits from the Generalized System of Preferences granted by several countries.[15] Finally, in 2002, the Dominican Republic expressed interest in negotiating a bilateral free trade agreement with the United States and Canada. More recently, in February 2003, the Dominican Republic signed a free trade agreement with Panama.

## 2.6. Investment regime

The Dominican Republic has put in place an investment and investor-friendly regime. The Foreign Investment Law (No. 16-95) was enacted in December 1995. With the exception of a few state-owned monopolies (such as hydroelectric power), the country allows foreign investment in nearly all sectors of the economy. Exceptions include disposal and storage of toxic, hazardous or radioactive waste not produced in the country; activities affecting public health and the ecological equilibrium of the country; and the production of materials and equipment directly linked to national security without authorization from the president. Other laws affecting certain sectors (such as banking and insurance) discriminate between domestic and foreign investment and remain applicable. For instance, there are sectors such as transportation, banking and insurance where foreign investment is limited to less than 50 per cent ownership but where domestic investment is fully allowed. FDI are subject to approval in specific sectors only, whereas in other sectors such as construction, joint ventures are mandatory.[16]

There are several cases of investors who have been involved in expropriation disputes. The Government of the Dominican Republic has committed itself to review these cases with a view to resolving them.

OECD INVESTMENT POLICY REVIEWS – ISBN 92-64-10509-3 – © OECD 2004

Although the Foreign Investment Law establishes a deadline for the registration of FDI, there is also no penalty for not registering or for being late since the registration mechanism is for statistical purposes only. The Central Bank and the Office for Promotion of Foreign Investment register the investments without previous evaluation.

## The tax regime

The Dominican Republic is one of the few Latin American countries, which has successfully implemented a comprehensive tax reform in recent years (*Ley de Reforma Tributaria* – Law No. 147-00 – of December 27, 2000). While many other countries in the region had to abandon, postpone or scale back their reforms, the Dominican Republic adopted in 2000 a flat tax on fuel, raised the value-added tax (ITBIS-Tax on the Transfer of Industrialized Goods and Services) rate from 8 per cent to 12 per cent, and increased selective excise taxes on tobacco and alcohol, which have also contributed to raise tax receipts. As mentioned in the section on the trade regime, the tax reform was accompanied by a tariff reform that slashed the number of tariffs by half and the maximum tariff from 35 per cent to 20 per cent *Ley de Reforma Arancelaria* – Law No. 146-00 – of December 27, 2000). However, in February 2003, the Government imposed by decree a 10-per cent surcharge on all imports – except food, medicines, raw materials and capital goods – for a period of 90 days, as part of a series of measures to promote austerity in an attempt to curb the depreciation of the exchange rate.

Key aspects of the Dominican tax regime include the following:

- Fiscal Amnesty: In 2001, a law on fiscal amnesty entered into effect. It allows companies and individuals to benefit from a fiscal amnesty for the payment of taxes (income tax, ITBIS and Specific Consumption Taxes) owed during the previous three years. Companies that do not take advantage of this amnesty and are found to have under reported their revenue, and hence paid less in taxes, may be subject to a fine.

- Advanced Payments: Companies must make a 1.5 per cent advance payment on the gross income tax they owe for the current year (this is payable monthly on the basis of gross monthly income). Companies specializing in agriculture (including livestock) are exempted from these payments, as well as companies with average annual earnings of less than RD$ 6 million pesos.

- Simplified Tax Estimation System: Companies or business people with income of less than RD$ 6 million a year may apply to benefit from a simplified tax estimation system, which seeks to make payment procedures easier. Under this regime, companies need to pay a monthly tax on income generated in the country. The tax rate amounts to 0.75 per cent on income of up to RD$ 2 million a year, 1 per cent on income between RD$ 2 to RD$ 4 million a year, and 1.12 per cent on between RD$ 4 to RD$ 6 million. Payments are to be made every three months.

- Income tax: The tax rate for juridical persons is currently 25 per cent. Individuals benefit from a tax exemption for income of up to RD$ 120 000 per year. Above this amount, the tax rate increases in proportion to the income, and as follows: 15 per cent for income from RD$ 120 000.01 to RD$ 200 000.00; 20 per cent for income from RD$ 200 000.01 to RD$ 300 000.00; and 25 per cent for income exceeding RD$ 300 000.01 per year. The employer must withhold this tax from the salary paid to the employee. These amounts are subject to inflation adjustments based on the Consumer Price Index calculated by the Central Bank. A tax rate of 10 per cent must be paid on income obtained in the course of business activities such as on fees and commissions. The tax rate is of 15 per cent for income from lottery games and 20 per cent for income from lease of property.

- ITBIS (Tax on the Transfer of Industrialized Goods and Services): This value-added tax applies to all goods and services, unless otherwise specified. For imports, it is levied on the c.i.f. value of goods plus customs duties plus the ISC (see below). For domestic products, the tax base is the net selling price plus related services, such as transport and packaging. As mentioned above, the Tax Reform of 2000 increased the ITBIS rate from 8 per cent to 12 per cent. Advertising services are taxed with a lower rate of 6 per cent. A wide range of agricultural and livestock products have been exempted from the payment of ITBIS, such as living animals, meat, fish for reproduction, milk products, vegetables and fruits for public consumption, coffee, corns, milled products, sugar, cacao, fuel and energy, books and magazines, as well as personal computers and accessories. Services excluded are education, culture, health, financial (excluding insurance), pension plans, ground transportation, electricity, water and garbage collection, rent of house, and personal care.

- Specific Consumption Tax (ISC): Various goods are subject to this consumption tax, which ranges from 5 per cent to 80 per cent. These goods include alcoholic drinks (beer, wine, etc.); carpets and rugs; caviar; luxury watches; electric household goods; electronic products; jewellery, etc. The ISC is levied on the c.i.f. value of goods plus customs duties.

### The FTZ legal regime and incentives

The FTZ legal regime is the most important component of the Dominican Republic's investment promotion strategy. Firms are tax exempted with respect to all domestic taxes, tariff exempted for all raw materials, equipment and machineries or any other type of tax during 20 years, and are granted a

OECD INVESTMENT POLICY REVIEWS – ISBN 92-64-10509-3 – © OECD 2004

50 per cent reduction for the payment of transit and use of ports and airports. Companies already established or which will soon establish themselves in those regions are granted a 50 per cent reduction for any other tax during the period of their 20 year tax exemption. FTZ-made finished goods are exported to the United States and the European Union duty free or with preferential duties under the Caribbean Basin Initiative and the Cotonou Agreement.

In an effort to diversify the type of investment the country has been receiving, the Government has licensed new zone franchises to private developers. One such example is the Itabo zone, where Westinghouse was offered to be both owner and exporter. Other examples include the San Isidro zone, built around GTE (now Verizon) and aimed at attracting firms in the electronics sector, and the Las Americas zone on information services.[17]

With respect to special incentives or "allowances" to corporations based on location (special economic zone), participation in a special scheme or compliance with a performance requirement, it should be noted that Law 28-01 of February 1, 2001 creates the Special Zone of Border Development and comprises the provinces of Pedernales, Independencia, Elías Piña, Dajabón, Montecristi, Santiago Rodríguez and Bahoruco.

The Tourism Development Promotion Act is an example of Dominican legislation aimed at fostering foreign direct investment because it provides for the promotion of tourism development in the areas and regions of the Dominican Republic which had previously only been marginally promoted as tourism hubs, and for the development of new tourism destinations in the provinces and localities that have great potential for tourism development. Law 158-01 also creates the Tourism Promotion Trust Fund.[18] Companies doing business in the Dominican Republic, and to which this legislation applies, are granted a 100 per cent tax exemption as follows:

a) national and municipal taxes for the use and issuance of construction permits, including the purchase of real estate, inasmuch as these are directly associated with the objectives of Law No. 158-01;

b) import tax and other levies, duties, and surcharges, including the value-added tax known as ITBIS (Tax on the Transfer of Industrial Goods and Services) as may be assessed against or applied to equipment, materials, fixtures and furniture necessary for the infrastructure that will facilitate the launching of the specified tourism project or venture;

c) national and international financing, if these are tax-exempt, will not be subject to penalties or taxation on the interests that may be generated;

d) natural persons and legal entities will be able to deduct or reduce taxes up to 20 per cent of their annual profits, as long as they are reinvested in a project related to this act;

e) the machinery and equipment necessary to achieve a high quality product (ovens, incubators, production and treatment plants, among others) will remain exempt from the moment of implementation of this legislation;

f) no new taxes, arbitrary charges or levies will be imposed during the tax exemption period; and

g) the benefits and incentives mentioned in this act are limited to projects that are implemented and/or constructed after this act has been passed.

Qualifying tourism projects, businesses or companies will enjoy a tax-exemption period of ten years, beginning from the date when construction work commences until such a time that the entire project is ready and the incentives can be implemented. There is a three-year deadline for initiation of permanent and uninterrupted operations of the approved project.

To be eligible for the incentives and benefits outlined in this act, all project proposals must provide documented proof of the following:

a) An environmental impact study that takes into account the type of project, the required infrastructure, the impact zone, and the environmental effect on the area. Small-scale tourism projects are exempt from this requirement.

b) A project blueprint as well as the preliminary engineering details of the same, prepared by a professional or by a certified firm of Dominican professionals. The counselling, consultations or participation of foreign specialists must be offered through local professional firms, which must be duly authorized and which will be legally responsible for the foreign expert.

c) Projects that involve the handling of large amounts of petrochemicals, and/or large-scale maritime transportation of same, must have a contingency plan to prevent and control any spillage.

d) Urban and municipal planning institutions and offices in the specified development jurisdictional areas must authorize such projects. In addition, applicants must submit a bank warranty to cover the expenses associated with environmental recovery if, through the project promoter's negligence, any harm is caused to the environment. Finally, no project may be located in any of the protected areas in the national parks, unless a study confirms that such a project does not endanger the preservation of natural resources or threaten the natural flora and fauna.

The businesses that are established in accordance with the benefits and incentives of this act must guarantee the preservation of all natural resources and due protection for the environment.

The State Agency for Tourism is responsible for ensuring and enforcing compliance with all provisions pertaining to the preservation of all natural resources and the environment during the construction and operational phases of the project. It is also responsible for informing firms should they fail to maintain service quality and quantity levels that allow these firms to enjoy the tax exemption status, and may make due recommendations for the suspension of the aforementioned incentives and benefits as necessary.

### Bilateral investment and double taxation treaties

In addition to the Foreign Investment Law and the numerous incentives available to the investors, the Dominican Republic has signed several bilateral investment treaties to improve the investment climate in the country and provide legal certainty to the foreign investor and his investment. The country has agreements in force with Argentina, Chile, CARICOM, Central American countries, China, Cuba, Ecuador, and Finland, as well as double taxation treaties with Canada and the United States. The country is also a member of the Multilateral Investment Guarantee Agency (MIGA) and the Overseas Private Investment Corporation (OPIC). Moreover, the country has ratified the Convention on Recognition and Enforcement of Foreign Arbitral Awards (the New York Convention), which provides courts a mechanism to enforce international arbitral awards. It entered into force in 2002. In March 2000, the Dominican Republic signed the Convention on the Settlement of Investment Disputes between States and Nationals of other States (ICSID) but has yet to ratify it. The country has also signed but not ratified the Inter-American Convention on International Commercial Arbitration.

## 2.7. Promotion of exports and investment: the Center for Export and Investment

In February 2003, President Mejía announced the formation of the Center for Export and Investment (CEI), as the product of the merger between the Center for the Promotion of Exports (CEDOPEX) and the Office for the Promotion of Investments (OPI-RD). As of April 2003, the formal creation of the new CEI was awaiting approval by Congress. The Center will count on the support of 22 commercial attachés in embassies abroad. The CEI takes over CEDOPEX, whose operating budget was increased from RD$ 14 million to RD$ 50 million, not including the RD$ 15 million it generates in revenues; and OPI's independent budget of RD$ 52 million. The new institution will find RD$ 117 million per year at its command for the promotion of exports and investments in the country.

OPI-RD, the Office for the Promotion of Investments of the Dominican Republic, was set up in 1997 with the mandate to attract both foreign and national investment in the country. It was created by an Executive Power Decree as an institution with administrative autonomy assigned to the Presidency of the Republic, which is in charge of the promotion of foreign investment in the country. OPI's main activities and functions are to promote and stimulate foreign and national investment in the Dominican Republic, as a means to contribute to the economic development of the country. OPI also directs investment toward those economic sectors declared as priorities by the Government or that are considered of priority and high benefit for the development and economic growth of the country. The Office works with the public and private sector of the Dominican Republic to design, finance, coordinate, supervise and evaluate new promotion plans with the purpose of increasing investment flows. It also recommends to the Executive Branch the adoption of measures to improve the investment climate such as changes to laws or regulations. OPI also conducts studies on FDI flows and trends, and on the impact of multinational companies on improving the international competitiveness of the Dominican Republic. OPI serves as a one-stop shop, a central point of contact for potential investors. Finally, OPI is also very active in negotiating investment agreements aimed at improving the investment climate of the country, and providing a stable legal framework for foreign investments and investors.

In an effort to reap the benefits of the synergy between trade and investment, the Dominican Government is in the process of revising Law No. 137-71, which created CEDOPEX in 1970. Merging CEDOPEX and OPI into a single institution encompassing both trade and investment will help optimize the strategies to increase investment and trade opportunities. The Government will be able to put in place a policy framework, which will foster the increase in FDI and exports, and encourage linkages between foreign investors and local exporters.

ISBN 92-64-10509-3
OECD Investment Policy Reviews
Caribbean Rim: Costa Rica, Dominican Republic and Jamaica
© OECD 2004

# Chapter 3

# Investor Perceptions

Investor perceptions of the Dominican Republic as a location for investment are quite positive. The state-of-the-art telecommunications infrastructure, which is one of the most advanced systems in Latin America, openness to foreign investment, political and macroeconomic stability, and access to global and regional markets are factors identified by investors as the key elements contributing to attract FDI. The country's geographic location is also considered a major source of competitive advantage by export-oriented firms such as those located in FTZs, which regard the country's access to regional and global markets as a strategic element in choosing the Dominican Republic as a location for investment. These firms have identified export incentives and FTZs, labor costs and worker productivity as strong factors attracting FDI to the Dominican Republic. For firms, which are market-seeking, the size of the Dominican market is one important factor. Moreover, investors recognize that there have been marked improvements, in general, over the past few years in the areas of crime (both street and organized), taxes, regulations, and "helpfulness" of the Government to the business community.

Among factors that need to be improved, investors indicate the high cost of electricity and the shortage of skilled workers and supervisors. Foreign market-seeking firms located outside the FTZs identified the education level of workers as a major weakness. Both elements can be addressed with appropriate reforms and in securing the resources necessary to carry out such reforms. They would contribute to attract more FDI and would also clearly benefit domestic investors. The enactment of the Electricity Law in 2001 was an important step in improving the framework for a more competitive electricity sector but as demand for power in this fast-growing economy doubled over the past decade, increased investment is much needed in power generation capacity and in the overburdened transmission and distribution systems. With respect to the labor force, the increase in the skill level of the Dominican workforce, which is perceived by investors as being "competent, trainable and cooperative", would help the Dominican Republic to compete for higher value-added foreign direct investment.

Other factors affecting the Dominican Republic's competitiveness for investment are government's regulations and taxes, including the unpredictability of Government's economic policy. The creation of a mechanism by which the private sector could provide continuous feedback regarding regulatory burdens investors are facing would help alleviate this

OECD INVESTMENT POLICY REVIEWS – ISBN 92-64-10509-3 – © OECD 2004

problem. The enactment of a modern Commercial Code (currently before Congress), eliminating burdensome requirements for the establishment of a business, and the removal of administrative barriers with respect to land titling and registration, and customs administration are other elements, which would improve the business environment for investors. Finally, corruption is another issue that should continue to be addressed, as it continues to impose significant costs on firms and makes business operations in the Dominican Republic difficult.

Table 3.1 provides a summary of investor perceptions in the Dominican Republic by investment location decision factors. The findings are based on a survey of 95 domestic and foreign investors in the Dominican Republic conducted by the firm SIGMA-DOS, with the cooperation of OPI-RD and FIAS (Foreign Investment Advisory Service) in 2001. All in all, 77 per cent of all respondents and 70 per cent of all foreign-owed firms interviewed for the survey declared that the Dominican Republic is an attractive or very attractive location for investment when compared to other countries in Central America and the Caribbean Basin. A significant number of respondents, however, 21 per cent, consider the Dominican Republic to be relatively attractive but perceive high risks and/or costs.

## 3.1. Recommendations

Within the next twelve months, a number of concrete measures could be implemented by the Government of the Dominican Republic, in the context of the National Competitiveness Plan launched in 2001 and with the support of international organisations such as the IADB and the OECD, to improve the investment climate in the country. These measures should include:

a) the enactment of a modern Commercial Code, which would eliminate the burdensome requirements for the establishment of a business;

b) the removal of administrative barriers with respect to land titling and registration, and customs administration;

c) the review of the incentive packages for investors, taking into account that the Dominican Republic may have to eliminate its export subsidy programs under the WTO Agreement on Subsidies and Countervailing Duties by the end of 2007 (unless WTO members agree on further postponement of the deadline to a later date). Such review should be undertaken using a cost-benefit analysis to assess the use and provision of these incentives in the country;

d) the establishment of an annual benchmark survey of investors views on critical issues affecting investment decisions; and

Table 3.1. **Summary of investor perceptions in the Dominican Republic by investment location decision factor[1]**

| | | Investment factors | | | | | | |
| | Overall | Ownership | | Location | | Sales orientation | | |
| | | Foreign | Domestic | Free zone | Non-free zone | Fully export | Part export-part domestic | Fully domestic |
|---|---|---|---|---|---|---|---|---|
| **Key elements** | | | | | | | | |
| Openness to foreign investment | 3.8 | 3.7 | 3.8 | 3.9 | 3.7 | 4.0 | 3.8 | 3.7 |
| Political stability | 3.6 | 3.5 | 3.8 | 3.9 | 3.5 | 4.1 | 3.7 | 3.4 |
| Economic stability | 3.3 | 3.1 | 3.6 | 3.4 | 3.3 | 3.4 | 3.5 | 3.2 |
| FTZ incentives | 3.2 | 3.0 | 3.4 | 3.7 | 3.0 | 3.7 | 2.9 | 3.1 |
| Overall incentives | 2.9 | 2.7 | 3.1 | 3.1 | 2.8 | 3.4 | 2.7 | 2.8 |
| Predictability of Government policy | 2.7 | 2.5 | 3.0 | 2.7 | 2.7 | 2.9 | 2.7 | 2.6 |
| **Regulations** | | | | | | | | |
| Labor regulations | 3.1 | 3.0 | 3.2 | 2.9 | 3.1 | 2.8 | 2.9 | 3.2 |
| commercial legal framework | 3.0 | 2.9 | 3.2 | 3.1 | 3.0 | 3.2 | 3.0 | 2.9 |
| **Infrastructure** | | | | | | | | |
| Infrastructure – telecommunications | 4.3 | 4.1 | 4.7 | 4.5 | 4.3 | 4.6 | 4.3 | 4.2 |
| Infrastructure – roads/ports | 3.2 | 2.9 | 3.6 | 3.2 | 3.2 | 3.4 | 3.1 | 3.2 |
| Infrastructure – electricity | 1.9 | 1.8 | 2.0 | 2.3 | 1.8 | 2.5 | 1.9 | 1.7 |
| **Competitiv.** | | | | | | | | |
| Access to regional mkt | 3.4 | 3.3 | 3.6 | 3.7 | 3.3 | 3.8 | 3.4 | 3.3 |
| Access to global mkt | 3.4 | 3.1 | 3.8 | 3.6 | 3.3 | 3.8 | 3.4 | 3.2 |
| Domestic market size | 3.4 | 3.2 | 3.6 | 2.8 | 3.5 | 2.6 | 3.4 | 3.5 |
| Labor cost | 3.3 | 3.3 | 3.4 | 3.6 | 3.3 | 3.6 | 3.3 | 3.3 |
| Labor skills | 3.0 | 2.9 | 3.2 | 3.4 | 2.9 | 3.6 | 2.9 | 2.9 |
| Cost of raw materials | 2.9 | 3.0 | 2.9 | 2.9 | 2.9 | 3.1 | 2.8 | 2.9 |
| Productivity and work habits of workers | 2.9 | 2.7 | 3.1 | 3.5 | 2.7 | 3.7 | 2.9 | 2.6 |
| Education level of workers | 2.5 | 2.4 | 2.6 | 2.7 | 2.4 | 2.9 | 2.5 | 2.4 |

1. Average ratings on a scale of 1 (very weak) to 5 (very strong).
Source: OECD.

*e)* the establishment of a clearing house where small and medium-sized local companies meeting some well-defined standards of performance would register and could become suppliers of the foreign (and local) companies operating in FTZs. Such a mechanism would encourage backward linkages.

Reducing corruption is another issue that should continue to be addressed, as it imposes costs on firms. The announcement in early 2003 of the creation of a new department – *Fiscalía Anticorrupción* – as well as other Government initiatives aimed at curbing corruption are welcomed steps.

# Notes

1. The Dominican Republic's gross domestic product (GDP) per capita based on purchasing power parity was of $5 700 in 2000.

2. UN Economic Commission for Latin America and the Caribbean (ECLAC), *La inversión extranjera en América latina y el Caribe: Panorama regional*. Santiago: ECLAC, May 2002 and March 2003.

3. State-owned enterprises are present in the following sectors: ports and water facilities; water supply and sewage; banking (for example, Banco de Reservas and Banco Agrícola); and in the transmission lines and hydroelectric generation facilities of the Dominican Electricity Corporation. The Government has nonetheless numerous shares in several privatized companies. See WTO document WT/TPR/S/105, September 9, 2002.

4. See WTO document G/SCM/N/74/DOM of January 8, 2002 where the Dominican Republic invokes Article 27.4 of the SCM. At their Ministerial Meeting held in Qatar in November 2001, WTO members agreed to postpone to 2007 the elimination of export or local content subsidies by developing countries under the SCM Agreement. Export subsidies were to be eliminated by 2003.

5. *Ley de Reforma Tributaria* (Law No. 147-00) of December 27, 2000 and *Ley de Reforma Arancelaria* (Law No. 146-00) of December 27, 2000.

6. The Dominican Republic has not been a major recipient of portfolio investment due in large part to its very embryonic stock market. The Bolsa de Valores de la República Dominicana (Dominican Republic Stock Exchange) has been in operation since 1991. A minimum reserve requirement with respect to foreign capital deposited in Dominican banks aims at discouraging short-term speculative flows.

7. These firms are: AES, Enron, Coastal, Seaboard, and Unión Fenosa. TRICOM, in which Motorola has a stake, ranks 15th. It is the second largest provider of long distance and cellular phone services in the country.

8. See Moran, Theodore H. 2002. *Foreign Direct Investment and Globalization in Developing Countries*. Washington, DC: Brookings Institution Press, p. 34.

9. The Dominican Republic has been a member of the International Maritime Organization since 1953 and has signed several conventions regarding maritime transport.

10. Maritime transport is governed by Law No. 3003 of July 12, 1951, Law No. 70 of December 18, 1970, and a number of decrees.

11. *Ley General de Telecomunicaciones* (Law No. 153-98) of May 27, 1998.

12. The Mejía Administration has recently attempted without success to end the blackouts by raising electricity tariffs.

13. See WTO document WT/TPR/S/105, September 9, 2002.

14. See WTO document WT/TPR/S/105, September 9, 2002.

15. Australia, Bulgaria, Canada, the Czech Republic, the European Union, Hungary, Japan, New Zealand, Norway, Poland, Russia, the Slovak Republic, Switzerland, and the United States. See UNCTAD document UNCTAD/ITCD/TSB/Misc. 62 of June 22, 2001.

16. An inventory of non-conforming (*i.e.* discriminatory) measures is being prepared by the Dominican Republic in the context of the Caribbean Rim Investment Initiative.

17. See Moran, p. 34.

18. Tourism Area No. 4, Jarabacoa and Constanza (Decree No. 1157 and 2729 of July 31, 1975 and September 2, 1977 respectively); Tourism Area IV Extension: Barahona, Bahoruco, Independencia and Pedernales; (Decree No. 322-91 of August 21, 1991); Tourism Area V Extension: Montecristi, Dajabón, Santiago Rodríguez and Valverde (Decree No. 16-93 of January 22, 1993); Tourism Area VIII Extension: Province of San Cristóbal and the Municipality of Palenque; the Provinces Peravia and Azua de Compostela; Tourism Area comprising the Municipalities of Nagua and Cabrera (Decree No. 199-99); Tourism Area comprising the Province of Samaná (Decree No. 91-94 of March 31, 1994); and The Province of Hato Mayor and its municipalities; the Province of El Seybo and its municipalities; the Province of San Pedro de Macorís and its municipalities; the Province of Espaillat and its municipalities: Higüerito, José Contreras, Villa Trina and Jamao al Norte; the Provinces of Sánchez Ramírez and Monseñor Nouel; the Municipality of San José de Las Matas; the Province of Monte Plata; and Guiguí, La Vega.

OECD INVESTMENT POLICY REVIEWS – ISBN 92-64-10509-3 – © OECD 2004

# Annex 1

**Exports**

In millions of US$ and as % of total exports

| | 1996 | | 1997 | | 1998 | | 1999 | | 2000[1] | |
|---|---|---|---|---|---|---|---|---|---|---|
| | US$ | % | US$ | % | US$ | % | US$ | % | US$ | % |
| **Free trade zones** | | | | | | | | | | |
| Textiles | 1 753.5 | 43.3 | 2 185.0 | 47.4 | 2 349.0 | 47.2 | 2 393.4 | 46.6 | 2 495.3 | 43.5 |
| Footwear | 264.6 | 6.5 | 310.6 | 6.7 | 348.5 | 7.0 | 357.9 | 7.0 | 268.8 | 4.7 |
| Electronics | 241.3 | 6.0 | 300.2 | 6.5 | 362.3 | 7.3 | 445.7 | 8.7 | 570.2 | 9.9 |
| Tobacco manufacturing | 235.5 | 5.8 | 280.6 | 6.1 | 329.4 | 6.6 | 320.4 | 6.2 | 329.9 | 5.8 |
| Jewellery | 145.4 | 3.6 | 178.9 | 3.9 | 239.8 | 4.8 | 280.5 | 5.5 | 459.1 | 8.0 |
| Medical drug products | 154.1 | 3.8 | 190.6 | 4.1 | 228.5 | 4.6 | 270.5 | 5.3 | 320.5 | 5.6 |
| Other | 313.0 | 7.7 | 150.5 | 3.3 | 242.7 | 4.9 | 263.1 | 5.1 | 326.8 | 5.7 |
| Total free trade zones | 3 107.4 | 76.7 | 3 596.4 | 78.0 | 4 100.2 | 82.3 | 4 331.5 | 84.3 | 4 770.6 | 83.2 |
| **Traditional** | | | | | | | | | | |
| Sugar and related products | 175.8 | 4.3 | 203.8 | 4.4 | 142.2 | 2.9 | 89.6 | 1.7 | 89.6 | 1.6 |
| Coffee | 64.1 | 1.6 | 67.9 | 1.5 | 67.1 | 1.3 | 23.8 | 0.5 | 33.0 | 0.6 |
| Cocoa | 64.7 | 1.6 | 61.0 | 1.3 | 87.1 | 1.7 | 24.7 | 0.5 | 26.1 | 0.5 |
| Tobacco | 51.8 | 1.3 | 91.2 | 2.0 | 63.3 | 1.3 | 53.8 | 1.0 | 44.7 | 0.8 |
| Nickel-iron | 218.8 | 5.4 | 216.5 | 4.7 | 132.1 | 2.7 | 143.9 | 2.8 | 237.4 | 4.1 |
| *Doré* | 48.7 | 1.2 | 27.3 | 0.6 | 15.5 | 0.3 | 6.9 | 0.1 | – | – |
| Total traditional | 623.9 | 15.4 | 667.7 | 14.5 | 507.3 | 10.2 | 342.7 | 6.7 | 430.8 | 7.5 |
| **Total non-traditional** | **205.3** | **5.1** | **216.8** | **4.7** | **232.4** | **4.7** | **284.8** | **5.5** | **352.2** | **6.1** |
| **Total other[2]** | **116.3** | **2.9** | **132.8** | **2.9** | **140.6** | **2.8** | **177.6** | **3.5** | **183.1** | **3.2** |
| **Total exports** | **4 052.9** | **100.0** | **4 613.7** | **100.0** | **4 980.5** | **100.0** | **5 136.6** | **100.0** | **5 736.7** | **100.0** |

1. Preliminary data.
2. Includes goods sold at port.
*Source:* IMF and Central Bank.

# Annex 2

## Imports
### In millions of US$ and as % of total exports

| | 1996 | | 1997 | | 1998 | | 1999 | | 2000[1] | |
|---|---|---|---|---|---|---|---|---|---|---|
| | US$ | % | US$ | % | US$ | % | US$ | % | US$ | % |
| **Consumer goods** | | | | | | | | | | |
| Durable goods | 380.6 | 6.6 | 425.3 | 6.4 | 541.1 | 7.1 | 542.8 | 6.8 | 631.8 | 6.7 |
| Refined petroleum products | 470.1 | 8.2 | 520.3 | 7.9 | 453.8 | 6.0 | 615.7 | 7.7 | 1 096.3 | 11.6 |
| Other | 871.5 | 15.2 | 1 080.6 | 16.4 | 1 173.6 | 15.4 | 1 210.4 | 15.1 | 1 459.2 | 15.4 |
| Total consumer goods | 1 722.2 | 30.1 | 2 026.2 | 30.7 | 2 168.5 | 28.5 | 2 368.9 | 29.5 | 3 187.3 | 33.6 |
| **Intermediate goods** | | | | | | | | | | |
| Crude oil and reconstituted fuel | 297.5 | 5.2 | 293.9 | 4.4 | 194.1 | 2.6 | 255.3 | 3.2 | 408.9 | 4.3 |
| Other | 1 002.7 | 17.5 | 1 175.5 | 17.8 | 1 452.0 | 19.1 | 1 532.1 | 19.1 | 1 622.6 | 17.1 |
| Total intermediate goods | 1 300.2 | 22.7 | 1 469.4 | 22.2 | 1 646.1 | 21.7 | 1 787.4 | 22.2 | 2 031.5 | 21.4 |
| **Capital goods** | 558.3 | 9.7 | 696.2 | 10.5 | 1 082.1 | 14.2 | 1 050.5 | 13.1 | 1 197.2 | 12.6 |
| **Imports into the free trade zones** | 2 146.3 | 37.5 | 2 416.7 | 36.6 | 2 700.7 | 35.5 | 2 834.3 | 35.2 | 3 062.5 | 32.3 |
| **Total imports** | 5 727.0 | 100.0 | 6 608.5 | 100.0 | 7 597.4 | 100.0 | 8 041.1 | 100.0 | 9 478.5 | 100.0 |

1. Preliminary data.

*Source:* IMF and Central Bank.

# Costa Rica

*Costa Rica has been very successful in attracting Foreign Direct Investment (FDI) over the past decade. Among the factors responsible for this success are a well-educated labour force, political stability resulting form the longest tradition of continuous democratic rule in Latin America and a positive record of transparency and government probity. This report details Costa Rica's success in attracting FDI, describes the positive impact that those FDI inflows have had in the process of the economic development of the country and provides a look at the leading business climate issues.*

OECD INVESTMENT POLICY REVIEWS – ISBN 92-64-10509-3 – © OECD 2004

# Preface

$U$ndoubtedly, Costa Rica represents a success story in the attraction of foreign direct investment (FDI). Not only have flows increased significantly in the past decade, but most have been new, green-field investment, in contrast with other Latin American countries, where part of the FDI has come from privatization programs.

Costa Rica's outcome is the result of several factors, one being the outward-looking development strategy it adopted in the early eighties, which combines unilateral measures to reduce tariffs with strong participation in bilateral and regional free trade agreements, as well as in the multilateral context. Currently, Costa Rica is working with other Central American countries to negotiate a free trade agreement with the United States. This will provide greater access to the most important market for Costa Rican exports. This free trade policy has been supplemented with a free zone regime that offers benefits to companies that make new investments.

In addition to its increased integration into international markets, Costa Rica has traditionally been open to foreign investment, providing international companies with the same rights as local ones. Costa Rica's success in attracting FDI is also closely related to the availability of a well-educated labor force, noted for its high quality and productivity. This is one of Costa Rica's main competitive advantages in attracting FDI, especially when rapid technological change requires flexible, fast-learning human capital. This offsets the relatively high cost of labor. The challenges, however, are equally important if Costa Rica is to remain as a competitive investment location for efficiency-seeking companies.

Other conditions such as political stability, the rule of law and transparency have further strengthened Costa Rica's position on the investment map.

Founded twenty years ago, Costa Rica's investment promotion agency, CINDE, has played an important role in assisting potential investors during their decision-making process and, once established, in maintaining close relationships with them.

Costa Rica has benefited greatly from FDI, mainly through the creation of jobs and the availability of a healthy source of financing for the current account deficit. There is great potential to continue attracting FDI in the future and maintaining these benefits. In a highly competitive context, however, where firms are dynamic and continually evolving to adapt to the market and changing technological conditions, only a well-defined and consistent strategy will allow the country to meet investors' needs. Costa Rica's challenge is to identify and focus on companies' critical location-driving factors.

This Business Environment Report provides a comprehensive and practical guide for the improvement of Costa Rica's investment climate, and should be taken into consideration by government authorities in their efforts to increase the nation's competitiveness. For instance, CINDE strongly believes that its qualified labor force positions Costa Rica as an ideal location for high value added services with excellent potential for job creation. However, specific efforts should be made to improve certain factors in the investment climate that are critical to this specific type of activities. These include English proficiency, computer literacy, and the cost and quality of telecommunications services.

The report also helps explain Costa Rica's success in attracting FDI, and provides a detailed look into the leading business climate issues, making it a useful tool for potential investors.

F. Tomás Dueñas
Chairman
Costa Rican Investment Board

ISBN 92-64-10509-3
OECD Investment Policy Reviews
Caribbean Rim: Costa Rica, Dominican Republic and Jamaica
© OECD 2004

# Executive Summary

Costa Rica is a small developing economy located in Central America, with a GDP per capita of US$4 083 in 2001 and a population of 4 million. Traditionally open to foreign investment, during the last decade, Costa Rican economic policies have been oriented towards fostering an optimal penetration of the country into international markets, mainly by expanding and diversifying its export base.

Within this process, foreign direct investment (FDI) has played a key role. Despite facing important challenges ahead, Costa Rica represents an outstanding success story of a small economy being able to increase and diversify its exports and attracting significant FDI inflows into its economy.

At the beginning of the 1980s, when the debt crisis revealed the limitations of the import substitution industrialization (ISI) model, Costa Rica opted for an export-led development strategy, based on the increase and diversification of its exports. As a result of this policy paradigm Costa Rica has become more effective in penetrating international markets. This has been reflected not only in the magnitude and composition of its trade of goods and services with the rest of the world, but also in the way the country has financed the excess expenditures over domestic savings. Costa Rican economic policy has entailed the adoption of fiscal incentives and the application of an exchange rate policy fully committed to maintaining the competitiveness of Costa Rican exports abroad. These elements, among others, have led to a more favorable environment for the exporting sector and foreign investment.

During the 1990s, Costa Rican exports experienced a significant change in structure, which has been mainly reflected in the considerable share manufacturing exports and trade in services have gained within total exports, gradually decreasing the dependence of Costa Rica's economy on traditional export commodities, such as coffee and bananas. During the last decade the balance of payments showed an quantitative and qualitative improvement, and the current account deficit came to be financed mainly by FDI flows towards the private sector. Indeed, during 1997-2001 FDI flows have financed on average 81.6% of the current account deficit in Costa Rica.[1]

Costa Rica has adopted a proactive policy towards attracting increasing FDI flows, by improving its human resources, reducing red-tape and favoring an economic policy which improves the country's business climate. Contrary to other countries in Latin America, FDI inflows in Costa Rica have not been associated with significant privatization programs. In fact, the pace of domestic economic reform since 1990 has been slower than in most other countries in Latin America – in particular in the field of privatization of state-owned monopolies in key services sectors of the economy such as telecommunications, distribution of electricity and insurance. This factor is gradually becoming a serious bottleneck in Costa Rica's long term development, and casts some shadow over an overall economic performance assessment which otherwise has been extremely positive during this period.

Despite the slower pace of economic reform, in particular in the services sector, since the mid 1980s Costa Rica has been able to maintain the internal stability during the reform process. The average rate of the GDP in real terms during the 1990s was 5.4% and the GDP per capita, 20.1%, while the average rate of inflation was 16.9%, after registering a median of 27.1% during the previous decade. At the end of 1996-1999, the inflation average decreased to 11.9% and the rates of growth of the real GDP and GDP per capita were 5.7 per cent and 18.1 per cent respectively. An old and chronic public debt (now reaching more than US$4 billion) has not only impeded the move to lower inflation rates to single-digit figures, but represents another major challenge that Costa Rica will have to face in the near future in order to provide the macroeconomic environment needed to regain the rates of growth experienced during the last decade.

Mirroring the situation in most parts of the world, in 2000, the pace of growth of the Costa Rican economy has slowed down, mainly as a consequence of a weak external demand for goods and services and a deterioration of the international terms of exchange. In that year, the growth of the GDP in real terms was 2.23 per cent, well below the 8.2 per cent registered in 1999, the GDP per-capita growth rate reduced to 6.5 per cent. Nevertheless, the inflation rate was just above the previous year at 10.2 per cent. In 2001 there were no signs of recovery. The sum of several factors (mostly current economic variables) meant that GDP grew only by 0.9 per cent, the rate of unemployment increased to 6.1 per cent and GPD growth declined even more, to 5.8 per cent while inflation prevailed at 11 per cent.

Among the economic factors explaining this decline after 2000 are the following. First, the effects of the recession of the US economy, by far the main destination of Costa Rican exports. Second, the fall in the prices of numerous exports in the agricultural sector. Third, a high cost in oil imports, and fourth a considerable reduction in exports of high tech products, motivated by individual decisions of major MTNs located in Costa Rica. The national currency, the "colon", has avoided major depreciations as the exchange rate has been subject to a policy of regular "mini-devaluations" aimed at reflecting domestic inflation.

Several variables indicate that Costa Rican exports and GDP growth will regain their momentum in the near future. The reactivation of growth in the US economy will lead to increased demand for Costa Rican exports, a trend which will likely be strengthened by the launching of negotiations for a United States – Central American Free Trade Agreement (CAFTA) – the conclusion of which is expected by December 2003. The CAFTA negotiations will certainly represent a very strong and positive signal for international investors. CAFTA will secure the access that most Costa Rican exports have enjoyed into the US market as a result of the Caribbean Basin Initiative (CBI). By establishing a legal framework regulating its trade and investment relations with the United States, Costa Rica is likely to become an even more attractive place for export-oriented FDI in the near future.

The success that Costa Rica has experienced during the last decade in attracting increasing FDI inflows into the high tech and services sectors represents a strong signal of the path the country could follow in the future. Indeed, with its high human development level and strong educational base, combined with its geographic location and proximity to the US market, Costa Rica is gradually experiencing a qualitative leap in its development. Thus, the need to undertake the domestic reforms and to continue strengthening one of the country's most valuable asset: its human capital.

Within this context, this report intends to provide an overview not only of the features of FDI in Costa Rica and the main factors behind FDI trends, but also an analysis of the multiple variables which affect its business climate.

OECD INVESTMENT POLICY REVIEWS – ISBN 92-64-10509-3 – © OECD 2004

ISBN 92-64-10509-3
OECD Investment Policy Reviews
Caribbean Rim: Costa Rica, Dominican Republic and Jamaica
© OECD 2004

# Chapter 1

# FDI Trends

## 1.1. Flows and stocks of FDI

From 1990 to 2000, FDI inflows into Costa Rica increased at an impressive average annual rate of 18 per cent (see Table 1.1).

### Table 1.1. **FDI inflows, 1990-2001**
Millions of US dollars

|       | 1990  | 1991  | 1992  | 1993  | 1994  | 1995  | 1996  | 1997  | 1998  | 1999  | 2000  | 2001  |
|-------|-------|-------|-------|-------|-------|-------|-------|-------|-------|-------|-------|-------|
| Total | 162.4 | 178.4 | 226.0 | 246.7 | 297.6 | 336.9 | 426.9 | 406.9 | 611.7 | 619.5 | 408.6 | 447.9 |

*Source:* BCCR, CINDE, PROCOMER, COMEX.

In 1990 total FDI flows into Costa Rica were US$162.4 million, and as Figure 1.1 shows, up to 1999, they experienced a constantly growing trend. By 1995 FDI flowing into the country reached US$336.9 million, representing more than double the figure of five years earlier. During this period, FDI inflows to Costa Rica peaked in 1998 and 1999 at US$611.7 and US$619.5 respectively, as the constant growth in FDI inflows was supplemented by significant new investments in the high technology sector. In 2000, FDI inflows decreased by 19.5% compared to the previous year, reaching US$408.6 million. FDI inflows increased again in 2001 to US$447.9 million, due to the persistence of the slowdown of the US economy.

### Figure 1.1. **Costa Rica: FDI inflows 1985-2002**
US$ million

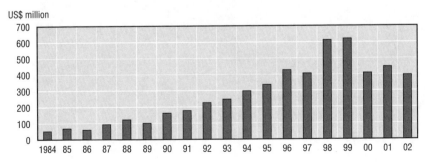

*Source:* OECD.

OECD INVESTMENT POLICY REVIEWS – ISBN 92-64-10509-3 – © OECD 2004

As will be explained below, given that most of the FDI in the manufacturing sector is export-oriented – and mainly to the US market – such decrease in FDI inflows can be explained in terms of the impact that the slowdown in the US economy has had over numerous export-oriented industries based in Costa Rica. It is worth noting, however, that despite the decrease in FDI referred to above, by 2002 FDI inflows to Costa Rica will still represent more than double the figure at the beginning of the decade.

Multiple factors explain the trend of increasing FDI inflows to Costa Rica during the last decade. One of them is the continuous implementation of an export-oriented development strategy that commenced in the 1980s. Among other objectives, this strategy aimed to diversify Costa Rica's export supply away from its traditional export commodities, i.e. coffee, bananas and beef. For that purpose, several programs including tariff and other fiscal concessions lured business towards non-traditional export activities such as manufacturing. Indeed, as will be explained in Section 1.3 below, the bulk of FDI inflows into Costa Rica has concentrated in that sector, in particular in manufacturing located in Free Trade Zones (FTZs). However, significant amount of FDI flows have also been attracted by the tourism industry as well as in the financial services sector – especially after State monopoly in current accounts was dismantled in 1995. In contrast, FDI inflows into traditional agriculture have tended to diminish during the decade.

Although in Costa Rica there is not accurate information to allow a clear distinction between green-field investment and reinvestments, CINDE – the Costa Rican Investment Board – has developed records covering key investments in certain sectors that provide some indication of the composition of the total FDI flowing into the country. On the basis of that approximate data, which should be taken only as indicative, Table 1.2 suggests that out of the total FDI flowing into Costa Rica during the 1997-2000 period, the most part was new, green-field investment. According to the partial data available, new investment represented almost 60 per cent of the total, while reinvestments represented 43 per cent.

Table 1.2. **FDI Inflows, 1995-2000**
Millions of US dollars

| | New investment | | Reinvestment | | Total |
|---|---|---|---|---|---|
| | % of total | | % of total | | |
| 1997 | 72 | 294.63 | 28 | 112.27 | 406.9 |
| 1998 | 49 | 300.72 | 51 | 310.98 | 611.7 |
| 1999 | 61 | 378.88 | 39 | 240.62 | 619.5 |
| 2000 | 47 | 191.12 | 53 | 217.48 | 408.6 |
| **Total** | | 1 165.35 | | 881.35 | **2 046.70** |

Source: BCCR, CINDE, PROCOMER.

Another indicator evidencing the significant growth of FDI inflows into Costa Rica during the 1990s is the total FDI inward stock, which, as Table 1.3 below shows, in 2000 was nearly four times higher than in 1990.

Table 1.3. **FDI inward stock, 1990, 1995, 2000**

Millions of US dollars

|  | 1990 | 1995 | 2000 |
|---|---|---|---|
| Total | 1 447 | 2 733 | 5 198 |

Source: UNCTAD, World Investment Report 2001.

## 1.2. Country of origin and destination

A quick overview of the origin of FDI inflows into Costa Rica is enough to discover the overwhelming importance that US investment has in the country. Between 1990 and 2000, more than two thirds of the total FDI flowing into Costa Rica originated in the United States. US predominance as a source of FDI is undisputed, as the second main FDI supplier, Mexico, represents a figure well below the US share. The pattern is complemented by several other sources of FDI, however, none of them representing a share of more than 4 per cent of the total.

Table 1.4 shows the top ten sources of FDI for Costa Rica in absolute and relative terms between 1995 and 2000. The table confirms the trends described above, placing the United States as the predominant source of FDI,

Table 1.4. **FDI inflows by country of origin, 1995-2000**

Millions of US dollars and percentage

|  | 1995 | 1996 | 1997 | 1998 | 1999 | 2000 | Total | Per cent |
|---|---|---|---|---|---|---|---|---|
| USA | 119.6 | 291.4 | 304.6 | 486 | 345.5 | 279.5 | 1 826.6 | 64.99 |
| Mexico | 80.4 | 36.6 | 21.7 | 21.2 | 92.5 | 29.3 | 281.7 | 10.02 |
| Panama | 5.9 | −4.3 | 0.2 | 1.9 | 69.2 | 26.2 | 99.1 | 3.52 |
| Canada | – | 8.6 | 8.2 | 34.2 | 35.7 | −2.7 | 84 | 2.98 |
| Germany | 19.3 | 4.4 | 5.4 | 10.9 | 7.5 | 10.3 | 57.8 | 2.05 |
| El Salvador | 0.7 | 11.6 | 13.9 | 0.6 | 15.0 | 15.1 | 56.9 | 2.02 |
| Italy | – | 1.5 | 10.3 | 0.4 | 8.2 | 6.6 | 27 | 0.96 |
| Guatemala | 5.2 | 0.7 | 2.1 | 1.9 | 13.7 | 2.4 | 26 | 0.92 |
| Spain | – | 0.8 | 1.5 | – | 0.1 | 21.8 | 24.2 | 0.86 |
| Taiwan | – | – | 3.8 | 6.9 | 3.9 | 2.9 | 17.5 | 0.62 |
| Others | 105.8[1] | 75.6 | 35.2 | 47.7 | 28.2 | 17.2 | 309.7 | 11.01 |
| Total | 336.9 | 426.9 | 406.9 | 611.7 | 619.5 | 408.6 | 2 810.5 | 100 |

1. Data for 1995 and 1996 FDI in the tourism sector was aggregated under the category of "others". A significant share of FDI under this category should be attributed to Spain.

Source: Central Bank of Costa Rica, CINDE, PROCOMER, COMEX and ICT.

with approximately 65 per cent of total inflows, far above the second main supplier, Mexico provided 10 per cent of the total FDI inflows during this period. The rest of Costa Rica's main sources of FDI represent significantly lower figures. Despite being the third FDI source for Costa Rica, Panama only represented 3.5 per cent of the total during the period, followed by Canada, Spain,[2] Germany, El Salvador and Italy.

The significant weight of United States among Costa Rica's main suppliers of FDI is no coincidence. The pattern demonstrates the new synergy between trade and investment as two complementing modes to service a particular market. The bulk of US FDI investment in Costa Rica is export-oriented, mainly to the US market. It is efficiency-seeking FDI that has found, in the internationalization of production, the best strategy to service its own domestic market. US enterprises have then implemented an international production system to which Costa Rica is gradually becoming integrated, thanks to the market-access concessions the country enjoys under the US Caribbean Basin Initiative. This phenomenon also explains the sectoral distribution of US FDI and the significant impact it is having in transforming Costa Rica's export supply, traditionally centered on export commodities, towards manufactures of higher and rising levels of technology. This point is developed in Section 1.3 below.

FDI originating in countries other than the United States have also increased their participation in Costa Rica during the last decade. That is the case of FDI from Mexico, Spain, and other Central American countries. However, it should be noted that contrary to the case of US FDI, investment from these countries has tended to be market-seeking, and particularly concentrated in the services sector.

In the case of Mexico, the negotiation of the Free Trade Agreement with Costa Rica in 1994 enhanced the interest of Mexican investors in penetrating the financial services market as well as manufacturing of some consumption goods. Likewise, in 1999 Central American and Panamanian investors also began to invest in the financial sector and retail services. Spanish investment in turn has been mainly focused on the tourist sector.

Costa Rica does not keep any official record on FDI outflows from the country. However, through empirical evidence and FDI statistics in other countries, it is possible to obtain an indication of the approximate magnitude of Costa Rican investments abroad. As shown in Table 1.5 below, UNCTAD has estimated that between 1995 and 2000 FDI outflows from Costa Rica amounted approximately US$29 million.

Table 1.5. **FDI outflows, 1995-2000**
Millions of US dollars

| | 1995 | 1996 | 1997 | 1998 | 1999 | 2000 |
|---|---|---|---|---|---|---|
| **Total** | **6** | **6** | **4** | **5** | **5** | **3** |

Source: UNCTAD, World Investment Report 2001.

Information on the geographic and sectoral distribution of Costa Rican investments abroad is scant. Empirical evidence shows also the existence of Costa Rican investment in the other Central American countries – in particular in Nicaragua – as well as in Dominican Republic and Panama. However, no detailed statistical evidence is available. The situation is different for Costa Rican FDI in Mexico. According to data from the Secretariat of Economy (SECOFI), between 1994 and 2000 a significant share of Costa Rican FDI outflows were geared towards the Mexican market. Indeed, according to SECOFI data, Costa Rican investments in Mexico reached US$9.1 million during that period, although empirical evidence suggests this figure is conservative. Mexican statistics suggest that Mexico captured approximately one third of the total Costa Rican FDI outflows during the second half of the last decade.

Information on the behavior of FDI outflows from smaller developing countries such as Costa Rica is extremely limited. Thus, the experience of Costa Rican FDI flows in Mexico is a case worth exploring in more detail. This experience provides evidence of two key trends. First, Costa Rican FDI abroad has focused on sectors that until the 1990s were not geared towards the international market. As shown in Table 1.6, out of the 47 companies with Costa Rican capital that are registered in Mexico, 38% are in commercial activities, 19.1% in services and the same percentage in manufacturing activities. Within the services sector, most of the companies are providers of professional, technical and specialized services, while those in commerce are

Table 1.6. **Sectoral distribution of Costa Rican FDI in Mexico: 1994-2000**

| Sector | # of companies | Participation (%) |
|---|---|---|
| Commerce | 18 | 38.3 |
| Other services | 9 | 19.1 |
| Manufacture | 9 | 19.1 |
| Financial services | 5 | 10.6 |
| Construction | 3 | 6.4 |
| Restaurants | 2 | 4.3 |
| Farming and livestock | 1 | 2.1 |
| **Total** | **47** | **100** |

Source: SECOFI – Data up to September 9, 2000.

OECD INVESTMENT POLICY REVIEWS – ISBN 92-64-10509-3 – © OECD 2004

dedicated to the wholesale of foodstuffs. As regards the industrial sector, the greatest concentration has focused on the production of plastics. This data suggests the gradual development of an increasingly aggressive and competitive business sector that is penetrating foreign markets not only via trade, but also via FDI.

The second trend that can be observed in Costa Rica's FDI experience in Mexico is that most flows took place during the second half of the last decade, that is, after 1995. It was precisely in 1995 when the Costa Rica-Mexico Free Trade Agreement entered into force. Thus, the behavior of Costa Rican FDI in Mexico is also indicative of the positive effect that international agreements can generate in increasing the level of certainty required to do international business.

## 1.3. Distribution by economic activity

Three major trends can be observed in the evolution of the distribution of FDI inflows by economic activity in Costa Rica during the last decade. First, the agricultural sector has suffered a dramatic decline in absolute FDI inflows, especially after 1992 when FDI peaked at US$113.8 million. In fact, as Table 1.7 shows, during 2000 FDI this sector registered a disinvestment equivalent to US$11.2 million. The decline of FDI flowing towards the primary sector is also evident in relative terms. From being the main magnet of FDI in 1990, when it attracted 54.8% of the total FDI flowing into Costa Rica, in 2000 agriculture became the sector attracting less FDI. This fall is associated with the

Table 1.7. **FDI Inflows by sector 1990-2000**

Millions of US dollars and percentage

| Sectors | Agriculture | | Industry | | Commerce | | Others | | Total |
|---|---|---|---|---|---|---|---|---|---|
| | $ million | % share | $ million | % share | $ million | % share | $ million | % share | $ million |
| 1990 | 89.9 | 54.8 | 48.8 | 30.0 | −0.5 | −0.3 | 25.1 | 15.5 | 163.3 |
| 1991 | 108.4 | 60.8 | 32.0 | 17.9 | 9.6 | 5.4 | 28.4 | 15.9 | 178.4 |
| 1992 | 113.8 | 50.4 | 51.9 | 23.0 | 5.8 | 2.6 | 54.5 | 24.1 | 226.0 |
| 1993 | 81.9 | 33.2 | 98.3 | 39.8 | 12.4 | 5.0 | 54.1 | 21.9 | 246.7 |
| 1994 | 42.7 | 14.4 | 167.9 | 56.4 | 48.5 | 16.3 | 38.5 | 12.9 | 297.6 |
| 1995 | 48.4 | 14.4 | 186.3 | 55.3 | 21.2 | 6.3 | 81.0 | 24.1 | 336.9 |
| 1996 | 34.6 | 8.1 | 257.4 | 60.3 | 35.5 | 8.3 | 99.4 | 23.3 | 426.9 |
| 1997 | 38.1 | 9.4 | 270.6 | 66.5 | 17.6 | 4.3 | 80.6 | 19.8 | 406.9 |
| 1998 | 41.9 | 6.9 | 423.5 | 69.2 | 39.3 | 6.4 | 106.9 | 17.5 | 611.7 |
| 1999 | 49.9 | 8.1 | 355.9 | 57.4 | 9.2 | 1.5 | 204.5 | 33.0 | 619.5 |
| 2000 | −11.2 | −2.8 | 296.2 | 72.5 | 17.4 | 4.3 | 106.2 | 26.0 | 408.6 |
| Total | 638.4 | 16.27 | 2 188.8 | 55.8 | 216 | 5.50 | 879.2 | 22.41 | 3 922.5 |

Source: Central Bank of Costa Rica, CINDE, PROCOMER, COMEX, ICT.

extremely low price commodities experienced in the international market during this period. This is particularly true for the banana sector, which traditionally used to concentrate significant shares of FDI inflows in Costa Rica and during the last decade has suffered a significant decrease in profits.

A second trend worth noting is in the industrial sector where FDI inflows have registered an astronomic increase during the period. Indeed, from attracting only US$48.8 million in 1990, by 1998 FDI in this sector was almost ten times higher, reaching US$423.5 million. Although decreasing after that year, by 2000 the sector still attracted US$296.2 million in FDI flows, more than six times the figure at the beginning of the decade. Further, during the 1990s, the relative share of industry in total FDI inflows increased from 30% to 72%.

The concentration of FDI inflows into the manufacturing sector in Costa Rica stem from two main variables. First, as mentioned in Section 1.2 above, Costa Rica is gradually becoming part of a scheme of international production – mainly from US multinational corporations. It is in the manufacturing sector where global production has been concentrated. Thus, efficiency-seeking investors, who represent a significant share of the investors investing in Costa Rica, tend to be concentrated in this sector. A second variable explaining the concentration of FDI inflows in the industrial sector is the harvest Costa Rica is enjoying as a result of investing in education for more than five decades. Nowadays Costa Rica's workforce ranks among the most educated in Latin America. This has provided the country with a comparative advantage in highly-qualified labor, a key factor explaining not only the establishment of manufacturing industries requiring a sophisticated workforce – such as hairdryers and fine apparel – but also the gradual conformation of a high-tech manufacturing cluster in Costa Rica.

Table 1.7 above also evidences a third trend in the evolution of the sectoral distribution of FDI in Costa Rica, that is, the significantly less dramatic growth of FDI in the commerce sector, a limited growth which also has occurred on a more erratic basis. Although registering overall growth, FDI in this sector has oscillated almost constantly during the decade. A tentative explanation for this trend might be associated with the limited dimensions of the Costa Rican consumption market, which does not make it attractive for market-seeking FDI in this particular sector.

A totally different situation can be observed in the category of "others" in Table 1.7 above. This category comprises FDI in tourism, a sector that definitively has shown a dramatic development and has lured significant FDI inflows into Costa Rica during the last decade. Indeed, in 2000 FDI in this item almost quadrupled the level reached in 1990. The positioning of Costa Rica as an attractive destination, politically stable and with a significant flora and fauna diversity has served the tourist industry well. In this sector, FDI is concentrated in European consortia, mostly from Spain. The peak in FDI experienced in this category in 1999, can also be explained in terms of the significant FDI inflows geared towards the financial sector, in particular in banking services. FDI flowing into the financial sector, mostly from other Central American countries, explains to a certain extent the final amount of FDI attracted in 1999.

## 1.4. Main foreign investors

The United States is home to seven out of the ten largest investors in Costa Rica, including the top 3 of them (see Table 1.8). It is worth noting that with the just one exception, all of the US largest investors participating in the top ten are concentrated in the export-oriented manufacturing sector, producing articles such as microprocessors, medical devices, textiles and hairdryers. The other three main investors among the top ten are from Spain and El Salvador, both of which are concentrated in the tourism services industry, and one from Panama, who has investment in financial services.[3]

Table 1.8. **Costa Rica's top ten largest foreign investors**

| Company | Country of origin | Sector | FDI US$ million | % participation |
|---|---|---|---|---|
| 1 | USA | Manufacturing | 91.23 | 22.3 |
| 2 | USA | Manufacturing | 39.43 | 9.7 |
| 3 | USA | Manufacturing | 30.24 | 7.4 |
| 4 | Spain | Tourism | 21.58 | 5.3 |
| 5 | USA | Manufacturing | 20.53 | 5.0 |
| 6 | USA | Commerce | 18.00 | 4.4 |
| 7 | USA | Manufacturing | 18.00 | 4.4 |
| 8 | Panama | Financial ss | 17.57 | 4.3 |
| 9 | USA | Manufacturing | 16.00 | 3.9 |
| 10 | El Salvador | Tourism | 15.00 | 3.7 |
| **Total** | | | **287.58** | **70.4** |

Source: BCCR, CINDE, PROCOMER, COMEX, ICT.

Out of the top 50 foreign investors in Costa Rica, 28 of them (56 per cent) are concentrated in manufacturing industries, 6 (12 per cent) in commercial activities, 5 (10 per cent) in agro-industry or agriculture and another 5 in various services. Further, the number of investors in some activities representing significant amounts of FDI, such as tourism and financial services, is surprisingly low. Thus, for instance, out of the top 50 foreign investors in Costa Rica there are only 4 investors in the tourism sector and only 2 in the financial services industry.

## 1.5. Main explanatory factors for FDI

In many ways Costa Rica has always been the exception to various political, social or economic paradigms in Latin America. The explanation of the significant surge of FDI inflows during the last decade into this small Central American country is, in many ways, another example of this trend. In many Latin American countries, during the 1990s FDI inflows grew at impressive rates after sweeping economic nationalist policies which discriminated against foreign investment were discarded, deep market-oriented reforms implemented and for the first time in decades, FDI was allowed to participate in different sectors of the economy. Furthermore, in many Latin American countries economic reform entailed the privatization of various key sectors that attracted important amounts of foreign capital into these economies.

Costa Rica deviates from this paradigm in two ways. First, although not totally exempt from the economic nationalistic trend, in Costa Rica neither economic policy, nor the legal system traditionally discriminated against foreign investment in favor of the domestic private sector. As a matter of fact and in general, Costa Rica has been a country open to FDI.[4] However, at the same time, and contrary to other Latin American countries, the surge of FDI inflows into Costa Rica cannot be explained in terms of sweeping privatization programs. The reason is simple: they have not happened. In fact most of the State monopolies in Costa Rica have not been yet dismantled. This does not mean that market-oriented reforms have not been implemented in the country, nor that they have not played a key role in fostering increasing flows of FDI. However, economic reform has mainly been geared towards the external sector.

Thus, the surge of FDI inflows in Costa Rica during the 1990s can be explained in terms of a clearly defined export promotion and diversification strategy, the success of which has gradually lead to the development of an investment policy based on a clear understanding of the comparative advantages of the country.

Although FDI has taken place in various sectors of the Costa Rican economy, as mentioned in Section 1.3 above the most dynamic sectors attracting FDI flows have been the industrial and tourist sectors.

### Market-seeking FDI in Costa Rica

Market-seeking investment in Costa Rica basically comprises three categories: FDI in certain manufacturing activities aimed at the domestic market, such as foodstuffs and cement, FDI in certain services oriented to the domestic market, such as retail and financial services, and FDI in tourism.

The first category of market-seeking FDI has been attracted essentially from Mexico. Mexican FDI has concentrated in foodstuffs, and construction materials, in particular, cement. In fact in 1999 Mexican investors acquired

OECD INVESTMENT POLICY REVIEWS – ISBN 92-64-10509-3 – © OECD 2004

one of the largest cement factories in Costa Rica. Mexican investment in this country has mirrored the trend in other Central American countries. Due to cultural affinity and geographic vicinity Central America is a natural market for certain Mexican enterprises. Furthermore, the negotiation of the Mexico-Costa Rica Free Trade Agreement that entered into force in 1995 also seems to have been instrumental in fostering these flows. This kind of FDI has been motivated by the need of obtaining distribution channels into the domestic market. Mexican companies have acquired local enterprises and used them to penetrate the market with their own brands.

The second category of market-seeking FDI in Costa Rica comprises services industries oriented to the domestic market. Central American investment in sectors such as retail and financial services have dominated this category. In fact, just between 2000 and 2002, FDI in the financial services sector has reached US$80.6 million. These resources have mainly come from Panama and Nicaragua. The opening of the financial sector in 1995, and in particular the dismantlement of the State monopoly in banking current accounts definitively has had an impact in enabling this FDI flow into the Costa Rican economy.

FDI in tourism is the third, and most important, kind of market-seeking FDI. Although not reaching the same magnitude as FDI in the export-oriented manufacturing sector, FDI in tourism experienced a substantial increase after 2000. In 2001 FDI in this sector reached US121.8 million, more than double the figure for the previous year. The estimates for 2002 are still very impressive, reaching US$101.4 million. During the last two years, tourism has become the most dynamic sector in FDI attraction in Costa Rica. Thus, the tourist industry in Costa Rica has not been affected by the terrorist events in the United States. Although FDI in this sector is basically originated in Spain and to a lesser degree in Canada, most of the tourism flowing into Costa Rica is from the United States.

In brief, Costa Rica has been able to exploit its natural endowments and fill a niche market as an ecological destination.

### Natural resources-seeking FDI in Costa Rica

Natural resource-seeking FDI in Costa Rica has been the less dynamic of all FDI categories during the last decade. Although increasingly active in the production of non-traditional tropical products such as pineapples and other tropical fruits, in Costa Rica natural resource-seeking FDI has been traditionally concentrated in the banana sector. Thus, the dramatic decline of this kind of FDI seems to be associated with the deterioration of the terms of exchange in most agricultural products during the last three years. Indeed, FDI in the agricultural sector dropped from US$49.9 million to a dis-investment equivalent of US$11.2 million in 2000. Although FDI to the sector resumed in 2001, reaching US$17.9 million, it is estimated that it will decline again in 2002 to only US$11.8 million, a figure that is almost ten times lower than FDI inflows into this sector in 1991 and 1992 (see Table 1.6 above).

## Efficiency-seeking FDI in Costa Rica

A fundamental element in the impressive performance that Costa Rica has demonstrated during the last decade in terms of its export expansion[5] and diversification has been the role played by efficiency-seeking FDI, which has become a key component of the country's development strategy. Since the beginning of the last decade, efficiency-seeking FDI has represented the bulk of foreign investment flowing into Costa Rica.

As in other countries of the Central America and the Caribbean, most efficiency-seeking FDI in Costa Rica is concentrated in the free trade zones ("zonas francas" as they are known in Spanish, hereinafter "FTZs"). The FTZ system began to be implemented during the 1980s, and currently approximately 300 enterprises operate in Costa Rica under this regime, generating around of 34.000 direct jobs. Although most enterprises operating under FTZ are located in one of the thirteen industrial parks in the country, a small number of enterprises of significant dimension operate outside those parks in their own premises. These enterprises are in fact the main exporters, comprising approximately 65 per cent of the total exports under the FTZ regime.

Without doubt, efficiency-seeking FDI in FTZs increased significantly during the 1990s. However, during the last two years there has been an important decrease in FDI in this sector, dropping from US$226.7 million in 2000 to US$131.1 million in 2002, (see Table 1.9 below). This trend seems to mirror the decrease in world-wide FDI flows during the period as a result of the de-acceleration of the world economy. Another important variable was the uncertainty generated by the obligation all developing countries had to comply under the WTO Subsidies Agreement, according to which, these countries had to dismantle all export subsidies – a category under which some benefits of the FTZs fall – by 2003. As a result of negotiations at that multilateral forum, WTO members opted to extend the original grace period for five additional years. This is an issue that will likely be brought to the current round of multilateral trade negotiations, so the grace period may be extended longer than 2008.

The decrease in absolute amounts of FDI in FTZs, and in its lesser relative importance during the last two years, may be misleading. In fact, the impact of efficiency-seeking FDI within the Costa Rican economy has been overwhelming. It can be better appreciated once its quantitative and qualitative impact over Costa Rica's export performance is observed. From a

Table 1.9. **Costa Rica: FDI for type of enterprises**

|  | 1997 | 1998 | 1999 | 2000 | 2001[1] | 2002[1] |
|---|---|---|---|---|---|---|
|  | US$ million | | | | | |
| Regular enterprises | 137.1 | 153.1 | 206.9 | 108.1 | 119.4 | 140.4 |
| Tourist Sector | 79.3 | 61.4 | 84.7 | 52.1 | 121.8 | 101.4 |
| Financial Sector | –0.2 | 22.1 | 93.4 | 27.1 | 29.8 | 23.7 |
| Free trade zones | 184.7 | 370.5 | 225.5 | 226.7 | 117.0 | 131.1 |
| *Draw back system* | *6.0* | *4.5* | *8.9* | *–5.3* | *0.0* | *0.9* |
| **Total** | **406.9** | **611.7** | **619.5** | **408.6** | **447.9** | **397.5** |
|  | Percentages | | | | | |
| Regular enterprises | 3.7 | 25.0 | 33.4 | 26.5 | 26.6 | 35.3 |
| Tourist sector |  | 9.5 | 10.0 | 13.7 | 12.7-27.2 | 25.5 |
| Financial sector | 0.0 | 3.6 | 15.1 | 6.6 | 6.6 | 5.9 |
| Free Trade zones | 45.4 | 60.6 | 36.4 | 55.5 | 39.5 | 33.0 |
| *Draw back system* | *1.5* | *0.7* | *1.4* | *–1.3* | *0.0* | *0.2* |
| **Total** | **100** | **100** | **100** | **100** | **100** | **100** |

1. Estimated figures.

*Source:* CINDE, PROCOMER, ICT, COMEX and BCCR.

quantitative perspective, during the second half of the last decade, exports under the FTZ regime rose exponentially in Costa Rica. While in 1995 those exports accounted for US$417.3 million (representing a 12.3 per cent of total Costa Rican exports) in 1999 they increased by a factor of eight, reaching US$3 591.9 million (representing 47.2 per cent of the total). Figure 1.2 below illustrates this trend. From a qualitative perspective, FDI in FTZs has been a key instrument in modifying the composition of Costa Rica's export supply. Nowadays, Costa Rica's main export products are no longer agricultural commodities, but microchips, medical devices and to a lesser degree textiles.[6]

Figure 1.2. **Costa Rica: exports under free trade zone regimes (1995-2001)**

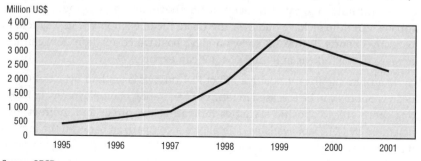

*Source:* OECD.

As Figure 1.2 above shows, despite the decline in FDI flowing into FTZs after 1999 which, as explained before is owed more to current economic trends than structural factors – by 2001 FDI flows were still four times higher than in 1995. These numbers allow the assertion to be made that the Costa Rican strategy aimed at attracting export-oriented FDI has been a success.

Three key factors, which are clearly understood by Costa Rican policy makers, explain the country's success in attracting increasing inflows of efficiency-seeking FDI. First, as efficiency-seeking FDI is export-oriented, securing preferential access to main export markets becomes pivotal. In this regard, Costa Rica has benefited from the Caribbean Basin Trade Partnership Act (CBTPA), which became effective in 1984 and was renovated in 2000. Under this law, with some key exceptions, most of the products exported from the Central American and Caribbean Countries receive duty-free treatment in the US. Thus, multinational enterprises based in Costa Rica can place the country within an integrated international production strategy aiming at the US market.

Second, providing a favorable environment for business has also been a crucial element of the strategy. Numerous variables interplay in providing international business with an adequate environment. Sections 2 and 3 of this report focus on them. Nevertheless, the traditional political and economic stability prevailing in the country, the strength of the rule of law, legal institutions and the low level of corruption have definitively played a key role in attracting FDI into the country, just as the tariff and fiscal concessions granted through the FTZ regimes seem to have played an important – although not always crucial role in this regard.

A third key factor of the Costa Rican success is its endowment of qualified labor at different levels of the skill spectrum. Indeed, even low skill labor is usually literate and able not only to perform more sophisticated tasks, but also able to easily learn other operational processes. This point is developed in Section 2.11 below.

## 1.6. Economic impact of FDI and linkages with the local economy

As initially suggested in Section 1.5 above, among the main positive impacts FDI inflows have had over the Costa Rican economy is its key role in fostering exports. Figure 1.3 shows a clear positive co-relation between the increase in FDI inflows and total Costa Rican exports.

Another significant positive effect FDI inflows have had over the Costa Rican economy can be assessed in terms of generation of employment. In Costa Rica there are no specific statistics indicating the direct and indirect jobs generated by FDI. Data available only allows a comparison between the growth of FDI inflows into the country and the number of jobs created during the same period of time. Although such comparisons only infer indicative trends and not

Figure 1.3. **Costa Rica: relationship between FDI and exports 1985-2001**

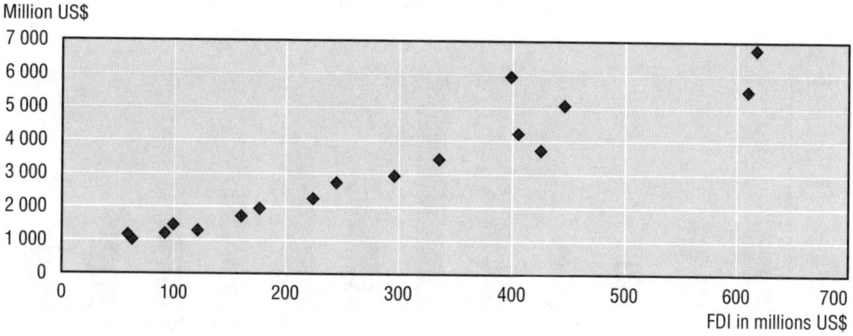

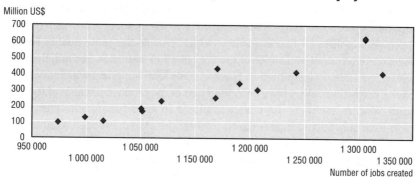

Source: COMEX based on data from BCCR and Procomer.

any causal relationship, data available suggest the existence of a positive co-relation between FDI inflows and employment generation. Figure 1.4 below illustrates that positive trend, showing how the number of total jobs in the country has risen substantially as FDI flows have also increased.

Figure 1.4. **Costa Rica: relationship between FDI and employment**

Source: INEC – COMEX – BCCR.

FDI has also played a key role in the overall macroeconomic stability of the Costa Rican economy. Indeed, during the last decade, FDI has become one of the major sources of cash to finance current account deficits. As shown in Figure 1.4, FDI has become one of the main instruments to offset the trade deficit in the balance of payments of Costa Rica. During the last 12 years, FDI inflows have represented in average 76.25 per cent of the current account deficit. In two years, 1996 and 1998, FDI inflows in fact were higher than the current account deficit, representing a significant source of fresh resources, and less volatile than other financing means, to the Costa Rican economy.

Figure 1.5. **FDI as percentage of current account deficit (1991-2002)**

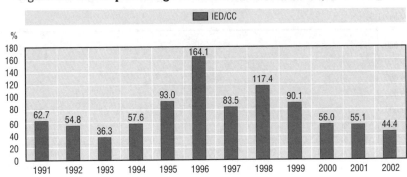

*Source:* BCCR.

Despite efforts to generate linkages between export-oriented activities and the rest of the domestic industry, spillovers have so far been limited. Although, strictly speaking, numerous local companies are already supplying TNC's, the truth is that most of their offer is related to non essential parts of the product, packaging materials, office supplies, etc. There are a number of factors that appear to be behind this lack of linkages. First, the production pattern of many TNC's is founded on a vertical integration that limits the possibilities of local suppliers to become part of the chain. Many TNCs source themselves from approved suppliers located elsewhere, which provide the same quality service/ raw material to similar facilities of the TNC in other countries. Second, there has been a technological gap hard to overcome for local suppliers which, to a great extent, keeps them away from becoming part of the production chain of the TNC. Third, venture capital is not widely available so as to facilitate initiatives that allow local suppliers to modernize or to close the aforementioned technological gap. And finally, there is a cultural dimension wherein local producers do not yet feel quite comfortable while dealing with TNC's demands.

Among the 4 842 enterprises that comprise the formal industrial sector in Costa Rica, 95% are SMEs[7] with less than 100 employees.[8] According to some recent studies,[9] these SMEs – that is, enterprises with less than one 100 employees – represent 28% of the Costa Rican GDP, 90% of the total manufacturing enterprises and generate 50% of the salaries and 80% of the jobs in the manufacturing sector. The national institute of statistics indicates that the workers hired by SMEs *with less* than 20 employees represent 26% out of the country's total employees. Further, it also indicates that private enterprises *with less* than 20 employees provide 51% of the total jobs in the private sector.[10]

The importance of SMEs in the Costa Rican domestic economy contrasts with their relative weight in the external sector. The majority of SMEs in Costa Rica are geared towards the domestic market, and those SMEs that in fact export,

OECD INVESTMENT POLICY REVIEWS – ISBN 92-64-10509-3 – © OECD 2004

only represent a modest share of total exports from Costa Rica. Indeed, despite comprising 62% of the total number of exporting enterprises in the country, in 1999 participation of SMEs in the country's total exports represented only 13% of the total value of Costa Rican exports. Further, most exports of these SMEs tend to be concentrated in agriculture and final consumption manufacturing products (mostly foodstuffs).[11] Furthermore, in most cases, SMEs target markets are located in other Latin American countries, and in particular in Central America and the Caribbean, rather than in the United States, Europe or Asia.

These figures suggest the existence of a segmentation within the export sector in Costa Rica. Two categories of enterprises can be distinguished. A first category comprises highly competitive enterprises that have successfully penetrated the most demanding international markets. This group comprises some Costa Rican manufacturing enterprises and all of the multinationals that have invested in Costa Rica in export-oriented production activities. Export activities of these companies evidence the following trends. They tend to:

- be the bigger exporters;
- concentrate the bulk of the value of Costa Rica's manufacturing exports;
- export manufactures with higher technological content; and
- be oriented to markets in industrial countries – mainly the United States.

The second category of exporters is comprised by most SMEs,[12] the export activities of which evidence the following trends. They tend to:

- target the domestic market, while gradually penetrating some specific export markets;
- be small exporters, relatively to the first category of enterprises;
- export agricultural products and manufactures with a lower technological content;
- be oriented to sub-regional markets, where geographic vicinity, familiar cultural consumer patterns, and less competitive environments increase their export possibilities.

Within this context, there is a need to implement effective mechanisms to internationalize Costa Rican SMEs, attempting to enable these enterprises to participate from the benefits of free trade and to compete in international markets. To fulfill this objective, several programs are being undertaken by several governmental agencies in coordination with private sector initiatives.

## 1.7. Future perspectives

In Costa Rica there were national elections on February 3rd, 2002. For the first time in Costa Rican political history none of the candidates reached the 40% of the votes cast as mandated by the Constitution to avoid a second electoral round. Thus, on April 7, 2000 voters cast their ballots again, choosing between the two candidates with the higher amount of votes. Mr. Abel Pacheco, candidate for the official party, *Unidad Social Cristiana* (a social-christian party) was finally elected by a significant majority of the total votes cast and was elected as President of the Republic for a four-year term. With the election of President Pacheco comes a team of economic advisors who share the basic market-oriented principles that have guided previous administrations. Thus, the export-led development model that has been continuously implemented since the 1980s will not likely experience any significant setback in the near future.

The little likelihood of major changes in economic policy unfortunately also has a negative side. Just like the three previous administrations, the new government will likely be prevented from fostering the dismantling of the remaining State monopolies in key sectors such as telecommunications, which are becoming a serious bottleneck in Costa Rica's economic development. Privatization is a controversial topic in Costa Rica, and no political group is assuming the political cost of explaining to the population the benefits of opening up those sectors both to domestic and foreign investment.

The current administration will also need to master the political skills required to deal with the most fragmented Congress in Costa Rica's history. Traditionally bipartisan, during the last election in February 2002, Costa Rican politics experienced a major transformation. Two new parties, *Partido Accion Ciudadana (PAC)*, with a left-centre orientation, and *Movimiento Libertario*, with a right-centre orientation, positioned themselves in the national political spectrum together with the two traditional biggest political parties, *i.e.* the social democrat *Partido Liberacion Nacional (PLN)* and the social christian *Partido Unidad Social Cristiana (PUSC)*. In the latest election no single political party obtained sufficient seats to dominate the Legislative Assembly. The ruling party, the PUSC obtained only 19 out of 57 seats, the PLN 17, the PAC 12, the ML 6 and two minority parties one seat each.

Thus, in this political scenario, a significant degree of political negotiation will be required in order to legislate. Although it might be early to tell, the Pacheco administration seems to have the capacity to deal with these challenges, as evidenced by the recent approval of the Costa Rica-Canada Free Trade Agreement by 53 votes of the Congress.

On the economic front, despite the current economic trend difficulties originated in the external sector, Costa Rica's macroeconomic indicators remain stable. Contrary to other countries of the region, as shown in Table 1.10 below, Costa Rica does not suffer a serious foreign debt problem, as during the last five years, foreign debt and its service has maintained manageable proportions.

Table 1.10. **Costa Rica: total foreign debt and debt service 1996-2000**

|         | Debt (US$) | As % of GDP | Service | As % of exports |
|---------|-----------|-------------|---------|-----------------|
| 1996    | 2 858.9   | 31.7        | 580.7   | 20.1            |
| 1997    | 2 640.2   | 28.9        | 583.2   | 17.8            |
| 1998    | 2 872.4   | 27.4        | 405.3   | 7.4             |
| 1999[1] | 3 056.5   | 19.5        | 533.6   | 8.0             |
| 2000[1] | 3 150.6   | 20.3        | 591.0   | 10.0            |
| 2001[2] | 3 326.5   | 20.9        | 469.4   | 12.3            |

1. From 1999 onward, the basis for the calculation is the 1991 GDP. Before 1999, the GDP used was that from 1966.
2. As of September 30th, 2001.
Source: Central Bank of Costa Rica, Census and Statistics Department, 2001.

After having an average annual growth rate of the GDP in real terms during the 1990s equivalent to 5.4%, mirroring the situation in most parts of the world, since 2000, the Costa Rican economy has begun to decline, mainly as a consequence of a weak external demand for goods and services and a deterioration of the international terms of exchange. In that year, the growth of the GDP in real terms was 2.23 per cent, well below the 8.2 per cent registered in 1999, the GDP per-capita reduced its growth rate to –1.2 per cent. Nevertheless, the inflation rate was just above of the previous year at 10.2 per cent. Although in 2001 there were not impressive signs of recovery, Costa Rica is not in the verge of a critical economic situation in the near term. Although several current economic factors led the GDP to grow only in 0.9 per cent in 2001, production did not experience a contraction, and although the rate of open unemployment increased, it was to 6.1 per cent only. Inflation prevailed at 11 per cent, a figure similar to previous years. The prospects for economic recovery are highly probable as most economic indicators will likely improve once the US economy overcomes the recession.

The prospects for increasing FDI inflows seem positive also due to the stability that those flows have maintained in the tourism sector – which in fact have increased despite the terrorist attacks in the US – but in particular due to the imminent initiation at the end of the year 2002 of the negotiations for a free trade agreement between the United States and the Central American countries. The establishment of a free trade area between the US and the Central American economies will definitively represent not only the culmination of a process of trade liberalization, but also the consolidation in the long term of the preferential access of Central American exports to the US market, a key factor behind the success of the investment policy of Costa Rica.

For establishing the basis for a sustainable economic growth, Costa Rica will, however, need to tackle two main challenges The first is to continue to strengthen its human capital which, to a great extent is enabling the country to attract the kind of FDI that most developing countries desire: flows in higher value sectors, in particular in high tech manufacturing and different kinds of services. To continue the process of strengthening the Costa Rican educational system is vital for the success of this developing strategy. The country has gone a long way in this regard. The challenge now seems to be concentrated in undertaking a qualitative leap: foster increasing English and computer skills literacy. The second challenge with which Costa Rica will need to cope is of an internal nature. The government will need to tackle its public internal debt, and continue the process of attempting to open the State monopolies in certain key services which have an impact on the competitiveness of the productive sector.

ISBN 92-64-10509-3
OECD Investment Policy Reviews
Caribbean Rim: Costa Rica, Dominican Republic and Jamaica
© OECD 2004

# Chapter 2

# Investment Environment

## 2.1. Structure of the economy

In 2001, Costa Rica had a GDP of US$16 381.9 million and a GDP per capita of approximately US$4 065.0.[13] During the last decade the Costa Rican economy experienced a significant positive growth. In fact, the country's real GDP grew at a compounded annual rate of approximately 4.6% between 1998 and 2002. During the last two years the pace of the growth rate has significantly decreased, from rates higher than 8% in 1998 and 1999 to 1.8% in 2000 and 1.1% in 2001. This information is further detailed in Table 2.1 below, which sets forth information regarding the respective growth rates for real GDP expenditures for the periods indicated.

Table 2.1. **Rates of growth of real GDP expenditures**

| | For the year ended December 31 | | | | |
|---|---|---|---|---|---|
| | 1998 | 1999 | 2000 | 2001[1] | 2002[1] |
| Private expenditures on final consumption (%) | 5.4 | 2.2 | 1.0 | 1.3 | 2.5 |
| General government expenditures on final consumption | 2.2 | 1.8 | 1.4 | 3.5 | 4.5 |
| Gross fixed capital formation | 25.5 | (4.1) | (0.9) | 1.5 | 7.9 |
| Domestic demand | 9.1 | (1.8) | 0.6 | 6.2 | 3.7 |
| Exports of goods and services | 26.7 | 21.3 | (0.3) | (9.2) | 2.8 |
| Aggregate demand | 14.0 | 5.4 | 0.3 | 0.7 | 3.4 |
| Less: imports of goods and services | 25.2 | 0.4 | (2.6) | 0.0 | 4.6 |
| Gross domestic product (%) | 8.4 | 8.2 | 1.8 | 1.1 | 2.8 |

1. Preliminary data.
*Source:* Central Bank.

Based on statistics from the Costa Rican Central Bank, in 2002 five broad sectors comprised the main share of the Costa Rican economy. These were the following:

● industrial manufacturing;

● wholesale and retail commerce, restaurants and hotels;

● transportation, warehousing and telecommunications;

● community, social and personal services;

● agriculture, forestry and fishing.[14]

OECD INVESTMENT POLICY REVIEWS – ISBN 92-64-10509-3 – © OECD 2004

Table 2.2 below shows in greater detail the relative contribution of each sector of the Costa Rican economy to the country's real GDP during the last five years.

Table 2.2. **Percentage of real GDP by sector**

| | For the year ended December 31 | | | | |
|---|---|---|---|---|---|
| | 1998 | 1999 | 2000 | 2001[1] | 2002[1] |
| Agriculture, forestry and fishing (%) | 11.2 | 10.8 | 10.7 | 10.6 | 10.2 |
| Mining | 0.1 | 0.1 | 0.1 | 0.1 | 0.1 |
| Industrial manufacturing | 21.9 | 25.3 | 24.1 | 21.9 | 21.7 |
| Electricity and water | 2.7 | 2.7 | 2.8 | 2.9 | 3.0 |
| Construction | 3.8 | 3.5 | 3.6 | 3.9 | 3.8 |
| Wholesale and retail commerce, hotels and restaurants | 18.9 | 17.8 | 17.8 | 18.0 | 17.9 |
| Transportation, warehousing and telecommunications | 9.1 | 9.0 | 9.7 | 10.5 | 11.3 |
| Financial intermediation and insurance | 3.5 | 3.5 | 3.8 | 4.0 | 4.1 |
| Real estate | 5.1 | 4.9 | 4.9 | 5.0 | 5.0 |
| Other business services | 2.3 | 2.4 | 2.8 | 3.3 | 3.4 |
| Public administration | 2.5 | 2.4 | 2.4 | 2.5 | 2.4 |
| Community, social and personal services (excluding public administration) | 10.9 | 10.4 | 10.5 | 10.6 | 10.5 |
| Less: financial intermediation services indirectly measured (FISIM) | 2.1 | 2.1 | 2.4 | 2.4 | 2.7 |
| Value added at basic prices | 90.0 | 90.7 | 90.8 | 90.6 | 90.6 |
| Less: taxes (net of subsidies) | 10.0 | 9.3 | 9.2 | 9.4 | 9.4 |
| GDP (%) | 100.0 | 100.0 | 100.0 | 100.0 | 100.0 |

1. Preliminary data.
Source: Central Bank.

Industrial manufacturing is a key sector of Costa Rica's economy, generating on average approximately 23.0% of real GDP since 1998 and accounting for approximately 73.7% of total exports and 19.3% of domestic employment in 2002. The most important manufacturing sub-sectors are food processing and beverage production, chemicals, textiles and the manufacture of wood and leather products. The rubber, processed foods and dairy products industries are also significant exporters. The manufacturing sector absorbs a large share of agricultural and livestock production as raw material.

The Costa Rican industrial manufacturing sector grew by 2.2% in 2002 as compared to 2001, primarily due to an increase in electronic manufacturing and growth in production in FTZs Exports from FTZ industries have experienced rapid growth in recent years. Indeed, value added exports from FTZs represented 35.0%, 53.9%, 50.5%, 46.7% and 48.2%, of Costa Rica's total exports in 1998, 1999, 2000, 2001 and 2002, respectively.[15]

The industrial manufacturing sector contracted by 8.4% in 2001 as compared to 2000, and by 2.9% in 2000 as compared to 1999, primarily due to a decrease in electronic component manufacturing by Intel Corp. resulting partially from its need to improve plant and equipment for the production of a new generation of products. In 2001, exports of electronic components from Intel Corp.'s facilities decreased 44.9% as compared to 2000 and by 35.3% in 2000 as compared to 1999. This significant decrease stemmed from the sluggish demand for electronic products resulting from the downturn of the US economy during this period.

The wholesale and retail commerce and hotels and restaurants sector, which captures a substantial portion of Costa Rica's gross tourism receipts, was the second largest sector of Costa Rica's economy from 1998 through 2002, generating on average approximately 18.6% of real GDP since 1998 and accounting for approximately 24.3% of domestic sector employment in 2002. The Government has developed a number of initiatives to promote tourism over the past 17 years, and such efforts have begun to render fruit as the tourism industry has experienced a sustained growth since 1997. This fact explains why the wholesale and retail commerce and hotels and restaurants sector grew by 2.2% in 2002, as compared to 2001, and by 2.1% in 2001, as compared to 2000.

Since 1996, when the sector surpassed exports of bananas, tourism has become the major source of foreign exchange for Costa Rica. Further, in 1999, this industry surpassed exports of all traditional products combined (bananas, coffee, beef and sugar) in 1999.

The Instituto Costarricense de Turismo (Costa Rican Institute of Tourism) is the principal governmental entity responsible for the promotion and regulation of the tourism industry. In 1985, Costa Rica enacted a law to encourage the growth of the tourism industry by granting this industry special tax exemptions, permitting accelerated depreciation on certain items and allowing duty-free imports of capital goods. As part of its objective to further reduce its fiscal deficit, the Government, after discussions with the tourism sector, eliminated certain incentives it had given to the tourism industry as of March 31, 1999.

Notwithstanding the elimination of these incentives, new investments in the sector are projected for the next three to five years.[16] In 2002, investments in the tourism sector reached approximately US$47.7 million.

The third largest sector of the Costa Rican economy in 2002 was the transportation, warehousing and telecommunications sector. The compound annual growth rate of this sector between 1998 and 2002 was approximately 9.0%. The telecommunications segment of the transportation, warehousing and telecommunications industry in Costa Rica is controlled by Instituto Costarricense de Electricidad ("ICE") and its subsidiaries, the sole provider of telecommunications services in Costa Rica. The growth of the sector during

OECD INVESTMENT POLICY REVIEWS – ISBN 92-64-10509-3 – © OECD 2004

the period has been primarily due to an increase in demand for telecommunications and cellular communication services of ICE and *Radiografica Costarricense Sociedad Anonima* ("RACSA").

The community, social and personal services sector of the economy is the fourth largest sector of the Costa Rican economy and consists of all health, education, entertainment, cleaning and domestic and professional association services. This sector grew by 5.8%, 3.4%, 2.6%, 1.8% and 1.9% in 1998, 1999, 2000, 2001 and 2002, respectively.[17] The rate of growth has been decreasing as a result of a slowdown in economic activity. The compounded annual growth rate of this sector between 1998 and 2002 was approximately 3.1%.

Agriculture, forestry and fishing is the fifth largest sector of Costa Rica's economy, which in 2002 generated approximately 10.2% of real GDP. In 2002, the agriculture, forestry and fishing sector contracted by 1.0% as compared to 2001, principally due to a reduction in market prices for the country's traditional export products. In 2001, this sector accounted for approximately 10.6% of real GDP, approximately 25.4% of total exports and approximately 15.7% of domestic employment.[18] The compounded annual growth rate of this sector between 1998 and 2002 was approximately 2.6%. During the last 11 years, Costa Rica has maintained a surplus trade balance with respect to agricultural products. Costa Rica's principal cash crops are coffee, bananas and sugar cane, the majority of which are grown for export.

In 2001, the agriculture, forestry and fishing sector increased by 0.7% as compared to 2000, principally due to an increase in the value of coffee and poultry, partially offset by a decrease in world-wide coffee prices. In 2000, the agriculture, forestry and fishing sector grew by 0.7% as compared to 1999, principally due to a 10.7% increase in the fishing sector, partially offset by a decline in the volume of banana exports as well as decreases in international banana and coffee prices. During 2000, traditional agricultural exports declined to an estimated US$877.8 million and imports declined to an estimated US$141.7 million.

This sector grew by 4.5% in 1999, in spite of adverse weather conditions including the effects of *El Niño* and *La Niña*. During 1999, traditional agricultural exports reached an estimated US$969.4 million and imports reached an estimated US$151.7 million. This sector grew by 8.2% in 1998 in spite of the adverse effects on the coffee, banana and sugar cane crops caused by Hurricane Mitch and other adverse weather conditions including *El Niño* and *La Niña*. The growth in this sector in 1998 was primarily due to increases in banana and sugar cane production.

## 2.2. Infrastructure

### Road and rail network

In Costa Rica there are two road systems that cover 35.877 km throughout the whole national territory. First, the national road system that includes the most important roads and covers 7 422 km. Second, the rural road system comprises roads of local importance that are generally maintained by municipal governments. According to data from the Direction of Sectorial Planning of the Ministry of Transportation, up to July of 2001, this rural road network comprised 28 455 km of roads.

Although there is no accurate data to determine the exact percentage of the national territory covered by the national road system, it is possible to affirm that, with the exception of those areas declared national parks or wild life refuges, the rest of the national territory is connected through the road network, at least up to the main town of each county and each district of the country.

Despite its extensive coverage, Costa Rica urgently needs an effective and operating system capable of enabling increasing private investment in the modernization and expansion of its road network. Since the debt crisis at the beginning of the 1980s, due to fiscal constraints, the capacity of the government to pursue and finance public works has decreased significantly. In a country where significant parts of the physical infrastructure supporting the productive sector remains in the hands of the State,[19] the contraction in public investment meant almost a complete paralysis in infrastructure development for more than a decade. In Costa Rica, public works projects are urgently needed to increase the competitiveness of the productive sectors and to facilitate the attraction of investment and new technology.

Given the tight budget constraints to finance public investment in the country, promotion of public work concessions has been identified as the means by which these urgent needs can be satisfied. Highways, railroads, seaport terminals, networks of sewer systems and other public works concession projects have been promoted. However, some of these projects remain stuck in the planning phase. More than four years after the Law of Public Works Concessions was passed amidst great enthusiasm and an ambitious list of projects drafted, the number of public works concessions awarded has been much lower than what was originally expected.

Some of the factors mentioned and associated with this tremendously disappointing results are the following: the inevitable learning curve of public officials and private sector with the new system; various deficiencies in the concessions law and the prevailing view among public officials and public opinion that concessions are seen as public contract and not a true partnership between the public and private sector. Last but not least, another cause that

OECD INVESTMENT POLICY REVIEWS – ISBN 92-64-10509-3 – © OECD 2004

seems to be affecting the proper operation of the concessions law is the profit margin of some of the proposed projects, which may be unattractive.

These apparent causes should be taken into consideration and solved, once for all, to enable public concessions to flourish in Costa Rica. Thus, the identification of mechanisms to enable this system of adjudication of public contracts to operate efficiently ranks among the most urgent needs the country currently faces in the field of infrastructure development.

There are, nevertheless, a number of projects – both proposed and underway – related to the construction, maintenance and repair of the Costa Rican highway system. In 1999, the government of Taiwan granted Costa Rica the funds for construction of a bridge over the Tempisque River in the province of Guanacaste, in the northwest part of the country. The funds were granted pursuant to a reciprocal foreign investment promotion and protection treaty between Costa Rica and the Republic of China (Taiwan), under which Taiwan may grant loans to Costa Rica in an amount of up to US$82.0 million for public infrastructure and other projects. Construction of the Tempisque bridge was completed in March of 2003, for a total cost of US$27.0 million. The access road to this bridge is expected to be completed in July 2003 at a cost of US$7.0 million.

The contract for the construction of the San Jose-Caldera Highway corridor, valued at US$150.0 million and linking the capital with Costa Rica's main port in the Pacific coast, was awarded to the Costa Rica-Argentinean company, Cartelone-Acosol, in December 2001. Construction of the highway is expected to begin in August 2003. In April 2002, the Government signed a contract for the US$125.0 million San José-Puerto Caldera highway concession with Cartelone-Acosol, a Honduran-Argentine consortium, which was the sole bidder for the concession. The National Concessions Board also expects to auction two concessions to construct two expressways through the outskirts of San José requiring an aggregate investment of approximately US$250.0 million.

In a clear contrast with the road network, Costa Rica has a limited railway system. Rail network coverage accounts to 278 kilometers distributed in three main routes: Limón – San Cristóbal (109 kilometers), Limón – Valle de la Estrella (59 kilometers) and San José – Puntarenas (110 kilometers). In 2001, a concession to upgrade and operate the country's railroad network was not awarded since the only bid submitted did not meet the terms of the concession. The concession was to upgrade, manage, operate and expand the national railroad network, which ceased operations in June 1995. The required investment is estimated to be approximately US$65.0 million for the 25 year concession.

### Naval and transport infrastructure

Costa Rica has two main ports, one on the Atlantic coast (Puerto Limón) and another one on the Pacific side (Puerto Caldera). These ports a serviced by approximately 22 naval companies with services to more than fifty ports worldwide. Both of two main ports are administered by state companies. On the Atlantic coast, the Board of Port Administration for Economic Development of the Atlantic Versant (JAPDEVA) is in charge of its administration while on the Pacific coast, it is the Costa Rican Institute of Pacific Ports (INCOP) the entity responsible for its management. Recently, the port on the Pacific coast, i.e. Puerto Caldera, is being subject to concession for private administration. However the adjudication process has not yet been completed.

Customs clearance in Costa Rica lasts takes between 24 to 48 hours, depending on the modality chosen by the importer to nationalize and withdraw the shipment from the warehouse. If the importer initiates the procedures before the ship docks in port (advanced dispatch), they become completed upon arrival, once the vessel transmits the information to Customs. Such transmission lasts approximately 24 hours and the merchandise becomes available to the importer once it is discharged from the vessel. In doing so, it can be subject either to documentary review or physical review. If it becomes subject to physical review, the procedures last 24 hours more.

The normal procedure entails the initiation of the paperwork once the merchandise has already arrived. In such case, the procedures last approximately 24 hours, including the review of the merchandise, depending on the speed of the carrier in moving the container. Such timing may be reduced to half if the merchandise is discharged at a bonded warehouse. Once the shipment has been nationalized, the carrier needs four or five hours to program its move to San Jose. Also, the trip from Limón to San Jose last six hours.

As the case of the road system, there are significant efforts to upgrade Costa Rica's port facilities. However, the process has not been easy. In 2001, the National Concessions Board and the Instituto Costarricense de Puertos del Pacífico (Costa Rican Institute of Pacific Ports) solicited bids for five concessions for the modernization of the grain and tuna terminal facilities located in ports on the Pacific Ocean. Two concessions did not receive any bids, one was awarded to the sole bidder, and the remaining two sought but lost appeals. Written agreements with each of the prevailing bidders are expected to be finalized in the second semester of 2003. Taiwan's Development and Cooperation Fund is also financing a project relating to the expansion and equipment of the Dock of Moin in Puerto Limón, in the Caribbean Coast of the country, with a US$15.0 million loan.

## Air transport infrastructure

Costa Rica has a total of 125 airports, 4 of them international and 31 private. The main international airport is the Juan Santamaría Airport,[20] located near the capital city of San Jose, and handling 92 per cent of the total international traffic. This airport is serviced by more than 12 airlines, directly linking Costa Rica with more than 20 destinations in the Americas and Europe. Currently, such airport is under the administration of a private company.

In 2000, *Gestión Aeroportuaria AGI de Costa Rica, S.A.* ("Gestión AGI"), a company formed by the international firms Airport Group International, Bechtel Enterprises and Bechtel Corporation and local firms Motorola de Costa Rica, SA, EDICA Ltda., CORMAR and Agencias Datsun, was awarded a 20-year contract for the operation, administration, maintenance, restoration, financing, construction and promotion of the Juan Santamaría International Airport in San José. Pursuant to the contract, the airport remains the property of the Government. Gestión AGI is responsible for the administration of the airport and is required to make capital improvements to the airport over the life of the contract at an estimated cost of US$180.0 million, of which improvements estimated at US$100.0 million must be made within the first three years of the concession. During 2002, it is estimated that Gestion AGI spent US$24.8 million on construction of the airport and that it will spend US$23.0 million in 2003 on additional airport construction.

Customs clearance at the Juan Santamaría Cargo Terminal is fast. The average clearance time is approximately two hours since most merchandise that enters or departs from that terminal is transported in aircrafts that remain in land for only a couple of hours. Importing procedures take about 24 hours, including withdrawal from the warehouse. Exporting procedures last approximately 8 hours.

## Infrastructure in telecommunications and energy

In December of 2000 Costa Rica had an installed capacity of 983 358 fixed telephone lines. This is the equivalent of 26 fixed lines per 100 inhabitants (260 per 1 000). In addition, there were 13 868 public phones, representing 3.6 phones per 1 000 inhabitants. Based on the National Census of 2000, 54% of dwellings had a phone.

In Costa Rica, telecommunication services are a monopoly of the state. There is only a sole provider, the Costa Rican Institute of Electricity (ICE). According to ICE, subject to the existence of appropriate infrastructure, that is, numbers and primary/secondary nets, installation of a telephone line can be performed in approximately three weeks. Waiting periods may be longer if such infrastructure is not available. Based on the Trade Policy Review Mechanism (TPRM) for Costa Rica at the World Trade Organization (WTO), in the year 2000 there were 73.2 faults repaired per 100 lines.

ICE has made important investments in fiber optic infrastructure. One example is its participation in the "Maya" cable network. The installation of the "Maya" underwater cable was completed in October 2000 and began operations in December 2000. The underwater cable is used to connect with other underwater telecommunications cable systems and has terminal points in Costa Rica, the United States, Mexico, the Cayman Islands, Honduras, Panama and Colombia. The total cost of the "Maya" project was approximately US$200.0 million, of which ICE contributed US$10.0 million. In April 2002, ICE completed a project for the installation of Arcos underwater cable for the transmission of data and voice at a faster rate than fiber optic.

Currently, ICE is working on the "Demanda Cero" project, which seeks to address the demand for domestic telephone lines. ICE's short-term plan to meet the country's demand includes the creation of projects to satisfy such demand within one year by, among other things, the installation of a fiber optic network between the borders of Nicaragua and Panama and the upgrading of the telecommunications network through the introduction of ATM technology. This project is expected to be completed in 2004.

ICE is authorized to sell 400 000 new cellular phone lines, and it has executed a contract with Alcatel which will allow ICE to acquire 400 000 GSM (Global System Mobil) cellular lines for US$151.0 million, payable in six years. ICE expects that the services will satisfy domestic demand and expects to open 15 000 cellular lines per month, beginning on December 15, 2002. This expansion is expected to double ICE's current cellular phone capacity.

Computer hardware is increasingly becoming part of the telecommunication infrastructure of Costa Rica. According to the latest National Census conducted by the National Institute of Statistics and Census on June 2000, there were 131 519 personal computers. Based on that same source, there are in Costa Rica 3 810 179 inhabitants, meaning that there are 34.5 computers per 1 000 inhabitants.

### Electricity and power

Hydro-electric energy is Costa Rica's main source of energy supply. In the year 2000, the annual production of electricity was 6 921 594 000 kwh. Based on National Institute of Statistics and Census on June 2000, the production per head is 1 816.6 kwh.

As of October 31, 2002, 89.6% of the electric power utilized in Costa Rica was generated by ICE. The remainder of Costa Rica's electric power was generated by other public sector entities and private sector power producers. As of October 31, 2002, the total electric power generation capacity of the Costa Rican electricity sector was 1 945.8 megawatts. In 2002, the electricity and water sector grew by 5.2%, which was greater than the rate of growth in 2001, due to a slowdown in the economy.

In 2001, the electricity and water sector grew by 4.1%, which was lower than the rate of growth in 2000, due to a slowdown in the economy. The electricity and water sector grew by 6.4% in 2000 as compared to 1999, principally due to an increase in residential consumption and the demand generated by electronic component manufacturing. This sector grew by 6.2% in 1999, principally due to an increase in residential consumption, an increase in public lighting services and the demand generated from Intel Corp.'s two plants. This sector grew by 8.7% in 1998, primarily due to the general increase in industrial manufacturing. Residential demand has been increasing steadily for the past several years. The compounded annual growth rate of this sector between 1998 and 2002 was approximately 6.1%.

There are important projects underway in order to expand the hydroelectric capacity of the country. The Angostura hydroelectric plant, located in the Turrialba, in the central part of the country, began operations on December 3, 2000. The Angostura hydroelectric plant has a generation capacity of 177 megawatts, and has increased the national interconnected system's energy capacity by more than 12.0%. The Peñas Blancas hydroelectric project, located in the northern part of Costa Rica, began operations in September 2002 with a generation capacity of 37 megawatts. The project cost approximately US$70.0 million.

In 2002, the Legislative Assembly approved a loan to be made by the Inter-American Development Bank to finance a project called the *Sistema de Interconexion Electrico* (the Electric Interconnection System) ("SIEPAC"). The entire project is estimated to cost US$320.0 million and the bank has agreed to lend an aggregate of US$240.0 million to Costa Rica, Guatemala, Panama and other Central American countries to implement this system. The Electric Interconnection System is expected to run between Panama and Guatemala and to begin operations in 2006.

During 2001, ICE obtained a US$154.0 million credit from the Japan Bank for International Cooperation ("JBIC") for the financing of the Pirris Hydroelectric Plant, located in the mountains south of the capital city of San José. ICE began construction of the plant in 2001. This plant is expected to open in 2007 with a generation capacity of 128 MW. ICE is also building a plant in Moín, in the province of Limón, in the Caribbean Cost, which is expected to open in 2003, with a generation capacity of 72 MW, and a plant in Boruca, located in the south-east part of country, which is expected to open in 2012, with a generation capacity of 832 MW.

## 2.3. Human resources

A high level of education across the different sectors of society is one of the most significant achievements of Costa Rica. Costa Rica's literacy rate is 95.5%.[21] According to the most recent World Development Indicators Report published by the World Bank (2002), 6 are the average years of schooling in Costa Rica. Further, based on data from the National Census 2000, out of 3 433 595 people in school age, 92.85% currently pursue studies at different levels. In Costa Rica there is a total of 7 156 primary and secondary schools, which means that there is one school per 532 inhabitants. As shown in Table 2.3 below, in Costa Rica there are more than three million students at different levels, the bulk concentrated in primary and secondary schools.

Table 2.3. **Costa Rica: Absolute and percentage share of population in school age pursuing studies at different levels**

|  | Absolute | % |
|---|---|---|
| Preschool | 111 934 | 3.5 |
| Primary | 1 814 407 | 56.9 |
| Secondary | 773 710 | 24.3 |
| Technical | 138 092 | 4.3 |
| University | 350 110 | 10.9 |
| **Total** | **3 188 253** | **100** |

*Source:* National Census 2000.

University level education in Costa Rica is highly developed and diversified. Based on the CONESUP (Private University Superior Education National Board) there are fifty-four universities: fifty private and four public. Two of them are focused on business, two on medicine, two on law, two on arts and architecture, and one in tourism. In addition, there are fourteen institutions that offer specialized training. Out of these fifty-four universities, four are public, and added together comprise 6 1385 students. These university centers are the following: Universidad de Costa Rica (UCR), Universidad Nacional (UNA), Instituto Tecnológico de Costa Rica (ITCR) and Universidad Estatal a Distancia (UNED).

Furthermore, there are forty-five institutes of higher education in Costa Rica. In 2001, twenty-three of them offered some sort of technical education.[22] There is a total of twelve public institutes of higher education that grant diplomas, technical or non-university degrees. Among them, there are the four public universities referred to above. The most common courses offered by the public institutes of higher education are focused on business administration (with different emphasis) and education. The other eight institutes are university colleges that offer diverse technical courses: cattle

OECD INVESTMENT POLICY REVIEWS – ISBN 92-64-10509-3 – © OECD 2004

raising, mechanics, business administration, information technology, natural resources, production, industrial training, etc.

In addition, there are fifty-three private institutions of higher education that grant diplomas, technical or non-university degrees. Seven of them are private universities, which offer as well other kind of higher degrees. The other forty-six institutions only grant non-university diplomas. The most common courses are: business administration with diverse emphasis, accountancy, audit, marketing, information technology, secretarial courses (bilingual or not bilingual), tourism, dental technician, and English.

The INA: *Instituto Nacional de Aprendizaje*, is the national training institute that offers technical professions, mainly for people who is already working. The INA is an autonomous institution created in 1965. Its mission is to promote the vocational development of men and women in all areas of production in order to stimulate the economic development and improve their living standards and job status.

Relatively to other countries, university education in Costa Rica has a moderate cost. Based on a research made by CINDE, the average cost for a Bachelor's Degree in a public university is US$1 460, while the cost for the same diploma in a private university is US$3 263. The study program for a Bachelor's Degree in a public university lasts at least 4 years, representing a yearly cost of US$365. The study program for a Bachelor's Degree in a private university last at least 2 years and 8 months, representing a yearly cost of US$1 224 the first two years, and US$816 the third year. The only one exception is for Health Sciences since the Medicine study program last 5.5 years, and each year costs in average US$3 450.

Regarding tuition costs to obtain a diploma in a institute of higher education vary significantly. Based on data obtained by CINDE, it was found that the cost of a non-university degree depends on the course and the institute. In a private institute, the average cost for the entire course is US$1 092. The average cost per subject is US$50 and the average registration fee is US$50 per quarter.

The figures referred to above clearly illustrate the significant advance accomplished by Costa Rica in education. However, despite those achievements, the country needs to reassess the role of education in the fostering the competitiveness of the country in an increasingly competitive world. Thus, another area where Costa Rica should devote attention in order to promote further systemic competitiveness of its economy is the field of massive education and strengthening the training of its current and future labor force. Despite having one of the highest literacy rates of the Western Hemisphere given its particular context Costa Rica must reassess its concept of literacy in order to include two urgently needed elements: English proficiency and computer literacy.

For Costa Rica to be fully able to integrate its economy into the international market, its population must undertake a qualitative leap in their education and be able to speak English and be able to manipulate at least the basic information technology skills. These two objectives become increasingly important considering the kind of FDI inflows reaching Costa Rica. Sectors such as electronics, business services and tourism require a highly skilled labor force. Within this context, English and computer literacy have gradually become a basic requirement to accede into any kind of professional, technical or even some sophisticated manual jobs. Thus, to provide the majority of the population with this basic skills has become increasingly important, not only as a means to promote better opportunities for all the inhabitants of the country, but also to ensure the competitiveness of the Costa Rican economy as a whole.

As far as the labor force is concerned, as of July 31, 2002, the Costa Rican labor force consisted of approximately 1.7 million persons, representing approximately 42.4% of the total population.[23] As Table 2.4 below shows, in 2002, the unemployment rate increased to 6.4% as compared to 6.1% in 2001, due to an economic decline, primarily in the manufacturing sector of the economy. In 2001, the unemployment rate increased to 6.1% as compared to 5.2% in 2000, again due to an economic decline, primarily in the manufacturing sector of the economy. However, in 2000, the unemployment rate decreased to 5.2% as compared to 6.0% in 1999.

Table 2.4. **Labor force and employment**

Thousands of persons, except percentages

|  | At July 31 | | | | |
| --- | --- | --- | --- | --- | --- |
|  | 1998 | 1999 | 2000 | 2001 | 2002 |
| Labor force | 1 376.5 | 1 383.5 | 1 390.6 | 1 653.3 | 1 695.0 |
| Employed[1] | 1 300.0 | 1 300.1 | 1 318.6 | 1 552.9 | 1 586.5 |
| Unemployed | 76.5 | 83.3 | 71.9 | 100.3 | 108.5 |
| Unemployment rate[2] (%) | 5.6 | $6.0^3$ | $5.2^3$ | $6.1^3$ | $6.4^3$ |
| Underemployment rate[4] (%) | 7.5 | $7.8^3$ | $7.3^3$ | n.a. | n.a. |

n.a. Not available.
1. To be considered employed, a person above the minimum age requirement must have worked at least one hour with remuneration or 15 hours without remuneration during the preceding week.
2. Unemployed population as percentage of the labor force.
3. Not comparable to prior years because of a change in methodology instituted in 1999 by the National Institute of Statistics in compiling data.
4. Underemployed population as a percentage of the labor force. Workers are defined as underemployed if they work fewer than 47 hours per week and are actively seeking additional employment or if they work more than 47 hours per week, but earn less than the minimum wage.
*Source:* National Institute of Statistics.

According to Costa Rica's 2002 Annual Household Survey, private economic activity employed approximately 1 586.5 thousand people in 2002, representing 93.6% of total employed persons in 2002, compared to 1 552.9 thousand people in 2001, representing 93.9% of total employed persons in 2001.

Despite the significant migration from Nicaragua to Costa Rica, the Costa Rican labor market has been able to maintain low unemployment rates. The majority of these immigrants find work in labor-intensive seasonal agricultural activities, in the construction sector and in the domestic services sector.

In Costa Rica, employment in the private sector is generally at-will, although employers must compensate employees terminated without just cause. Such compensation includes a notice of dismissal and a severance payment bonus based on the number of years of service.

The Constitution requires that minimum wages be fixed in each sector. Subject to this limitation, employers and employees are free to set wages and salaries. Employees may enter into collective agreement mechanisms and direct arrangements for collective bargaining of their salaries or may make use of wages and salary arbitration mechanisms. Costa Rican law provides protection against the dismissal of pregnant women and provides additional employment benefits to the disabled.

Public sector employees may be terminated only for just cause. Wages and salaries of public sector employees are subject to two annual cost of living adjustments. Since 1978, Costa Rican law has prohibited collective bargaining by public sector employees, except in specific institutions which had collective bargaining agreements in effect prior to 1978. In addition, the Supreme Court eliminated arbitration of public-sector employment disputes in 1993.

In Costa Rica membership in labor organisations is limited. Membership in unions as a percentage of the total number of employed persons decreased from 15.5% (160 166 persons) in 1992 to 11.9% (185 075 persons) in 2001. More Costa Ricans participate in *Asociaciones Solidaristas* (Solidarity Associations) ("Solidarity Associations"). Membership in Solidarity Associations as a percentage of the total number of employed persons increased from approximately 14.9% (170 406 persons) in 1996 to 15.9% (251 833 persons) in 2002. This increase in membership in Solidarity Associations is primarily because Solidarity Associations are permitted by law to collect in advance certain amounts of money related to severance payments from employers to be administered for the benefit of workers, who also contribute a percentage of their wages on a monthly basis to the Solidarity Associations.

In 1996, in reaction to pension reforms which required teachers to make increased contributions to the pension system, the teachers union engaged in a strike which lasted for six weeks. There has been no other significant labor dispute since 1982.[24] In 2000, some members of the unions representing the employees of ICE and certain other public sector unions demonstrated in reaction to the preliminary approval of legislation regarding the restructuring of ICE. This subject may remain politically sensitive in the near future.

In Costa Rica, wages are specified on a monthly basis, with the exception of the minimum wage, which is specified per day. Therefore, in order to calculate a per hour rate, the monthly total is divided by 48 (amount of regular working hours in a week) and then multiplied by 4.33 (amount of weeks in a month). Thus, the equation is as follows: monthly wage/(48 * 4.33). In average, hourly US$ earnings in manufacturing 2000 was equivalent to US$1.62.[25] Table 2.5 below illustrates the evolution of nominal wages during the last five years in Costa Rica.

Table 2.5. **Average monthly wages**
In US dollars

| | As of June 30 | | | | |
|---|---|---|---|---|---|
| | 1998 | 1999 | 2000 | 2001 | 2002 |
| Private sector | 342.8 | 359.6 | 373.0 | 384.1 | 386.1 |
| Agriculture | 285.8 | 294.4 | 288.0 | 280.7 | 275.7 |
| Industrial manufacturing | 384.7 | 410.1 | 430.7 | 451.0 | 467.1 |

Source: Central Bank, based on information of the Caja Costarricense del Seguro Social ("CCSS").

In Costa Rica several guarantees apply to hiring and firing practices. Currently, there are only two requirements for hiring. The first one is an age minimum that employers must observe. Since legal age is acquired at 18, employees aged 15 to 17 years old need a special permit from the National Childhood Board to work. The second one is related to the work of foreigners, who require a working visa that, like in many countries, may not be easily awarded to non-management employees, especially if there are people in the country able to perform the job.

As to firing practices, an employer may terminate an employment contract with or without just cause. When termination occurs without just cause, the employee is entitled to severance indemnities including the following:

● Advanced Notice: both the employer and the employee are entitled to up to one-month advance notice, prior to termination. Instead of giving advance notice, the employer or employee, as the case may be, has the option to pay an equivalent amount of salary.

● Termination indemnification: upon termination without cause by the employer, employees have the right to one month of salary per year during which the employment relationship has been in effect, up to eight years.

OECD INVESTMENT POLICY REVIEWS – ISBN 92-64-10509-3 – © OECD 2004

The indemnification amount is calculated on the basis of an average of the last six monthly salaries paid.

❖ Regardless of the cause of termination, employees are entitled to get paid any outstanding proportion of the mandatory 13th month bonus, as well as any accrued vacation days.

In those cases where there is just cause, the employee is entitled to the payment of wages, proportional vacation time and Christmas bonus. This bonus ("aguinaldo") is an additional one-month salary that must be paid to all employees after one year of employment. It is payable each year during the first twenty days of December. If an employee has not worked for a full year, the bonus must be paid proportionally.

Just causes for termination are specifically listed in the Labor Code, and they include physical or moral acts or libel committed against another worker or employer during and out of working hours; criminal acts or property damage; endangering security and working conditions; unauthorized release of confidential information; and disobedience of instructions or orders.

Foreign individuals without residency status and/or labor permit are not allowed to work in Costa Rica. Local and foreign entities doing business in Costa Rica may apply for special authorization from the Immigration Office to bring temporary workers, namely high-ranked executives and/or technicians, into the country. In practice, local authorities are flexible in granting work permits to qualified foreign workers.

As regards to immigration rules applicable to foreign workers, in the case of non residents, the company asks for a temporary work permit at the Immigration Department, previous to the employee's arrival into the country. The expiration of the permit will be defined by the type of occupation and other considerations. Residents have nothing more to comply with.[26]

## 2.4. Public governance: transparency, integrity, and rule of law

Costa Rica has a long tradition for the respect of the rule of law and democratic rule. Constitutional mechanisms for the orderly transfer of power from one government to another are very clear, established and accepted. The current Political Constitution, enacted in 1949, establishes in Article 134 that the Presidential term will last for four years and that actions that violate the alternating of power will imply betrayal to the Republic. Moreover, Article 149 establishes that the President of the Republic along with the Ministers of Government will be jointly responsible when they attempt against the principles of alternating in the exercise of the Presidency or in the free presidential succession. In practice, an orderly transfer of power every four years has taken place since the Constitution was enacted.

Costa Rica political system is a representative democracy with three different branches: executive, legislative and judicial. The president and two vice-presidents run on the same ticket and are elected for a four year-term. In late March 2003, the Costa Rican Supreme court overruled Article 50 of the Constitution, which prohibited presidential election thus creating the possibility for re-election. Elections for electing the members of the Legislative Assembly also take place every four years, on the same day of the presidential election. The Legislative Assembly is unicameral and comprises 57 representatives "*diputados*" who cannot be re-elected for consecutive terms. The Judicial System is headed by the Supreme Court that comprises 22 justices appointed by the Legislative Assembly who are considered elected unless a two-thirds majority of Congress decides otherwise.

Effectiveness of the political system in formulating and executing policy during the last administration (1998-2002) could only be rated as moderate. Several variables explain this assertion. One of the most important is related to the composition of Congress. During this term, there were more political parties represented at the Legislative Assembly than ever before, making it very difficult to achieve agreements on critical issues. Further, as the official party did not have a majority, it required the support from other parties even for those projects that only required simple majority. As a result, chances for the Executive Branch to obtain approval and support for many projects became considerably difficult.

The lack of a clearly recognized hegemonic leader in the opposition party, due to internal divisions, exacerbated this difficult governance situation. Thus, the administration had trouble finding a counterpart with whom to negotiate in Congress. Consequently, it was very difficult for the administration to implement key bills aimed at modernizing and deepening the market-oriented reforms initially undertaken at the beginning of the decade. In fact, several proposals aiming at opening up the energy/telecommunications sectors had to be withdrawn due this situation.

In spite of this very complex political context, important projects such as the "*Ley de Concesión de Obra Pública*" – which allowed for the concession of the administration of the International Airport and the construction of a new terminal to private investors-, or the "*Ley de Protección al Trabajador*" – which introduced important changes to the pension regime – were enacted during this term. Moreover, free trade agreements with Chile, Canada and the Dominican Republic seeking to increase and improve market access to Costa Rican products have been signed by the current Administration. Two of them have been already approved by Congress and the third is expected to be approved soon.

On February 3rd, 2002, there were national elections to appoint a new President and new members of Congress. As to the election of members to Congress, once again it came out highly divided. In fact, the allocation of seats in the parliament became even more fractioned than before, emerging not two, but four main political forces. Thus dynamics that prevailed during the last administration may continue due to this dispersion of power. However, the new Congress was inaugurated on May, and it may be too early to predict the evolution of the political dynamics.

In Costa Rica, the quality of the bureaucracy and its ability to carry out government policy is also moderate. However, important efforts are being pursued to simplify and reduce business-related red tape. In 1998, the "*Oficina de Simplificación de Trámites*" was created in order to streamline and facilitate business in the country. The success achieved by this office in the short period that has passed by since it was created has been very significant. Some of the most important goals achieved by this office are, among others, the following:

1. Close coordination between institutions involved in the attraction and establishment in the country of foreign investors: it has significantly simplified the procedures to be followed in order to start up operations.

2. Improvements introduced to the Free Zone and Active Finishing Regimes: it allows companies to handle their operations more adequately.

3. Clarification of procedures and paper work for the registration of fertilisers and pesticides: it allows companies to save time and money.

4. Training offered to the municipalities: it enables them to perform adequately their functions.

5. Simplification of the procedures for local purchases for companies in Free Zones.

6. Elimination of unnecessary requirements to import machinery and raw materials.

7. Clarification of the procedures to obtain municipal construction permits.

8. Breaking up of the monopoly that neglected the import of fertilisers, pesticides and animal feeding products.

Furthermore, the recent enactment of the *Law for the Protection of the Citizen*, which seeks to remove all unnecessary requirements to conduct business, may be perceived as a commitment to continue simplifying and improving the business climate.

Costa Rica's enjoys a positive record in terms of transparency and government probity. As Table 2.6 shows, in the Americas, Costa Rica ranks among the top four countries with more transparent and probe administrations together with Chile, Trinidad and Tobago and Uruguay.

Table 2.6. **2001 corruption perceptions index for Latin American and Caribbean countries**

|  | Rank | Score |
|---|---|---|
| Chile | 18 | 7.5 |
| Trinidad and Tobago | 32 | 5.3 |
| Uruguay | 35 | 5.1 |
| **Costa Rica** | **40** | **4.5** |
| Peru | 44 | 4.1 |
| Brazil | 46 | 4.0 |
| Colombia | 50 | 3.8 |
| Mexico | 51 | 3.7 |
| Panama | 52 | 3.7 |
| El Salvador | 55 | 3.6 |
| Argentina | 57 | 3.5 |
| Dominican Republic | 63 | 3.1 |
| Guatemala | 65 | 2.9 |
| Venezuela | 70 | 2.8 |
| Honduras | 71 | 2.7 |
| Nicaragua | 78 | 2.4 |
| Ecuador | 79 | 2.3 |
| Bolivia | 85 | 2.0 |

Source: Transparency International (www.transparency.org).

In Costa Rica the Constitution and certain legal codes rule and sanction certain conducts as white collar crimes. However, there is no specific law focused on white-collar crimes. In Congress there is a bill entitled "Law Against Embezzlement and Corruption", awaiting second debate, which deals specifically with this particular kind of criminal acts.

Although perceived as a problem by the Costa Rican public opinion, in the country there is no systematized data on the number of cases related with white-collar corruption brought before national courts, nor on the number of times that such kind of trials have ended in effective sanctions. However, empirical evidence suggests that the judicial system has been able to reach and successfully trial a significant number of important political figures. Paradoxically, this apparent success has generated a perception in the public that corruption in the public sector is widely diffused.

Indeed, based on the 2001 Report published by the Inter American Development Bank named "The Business of Growth: Economic and Social Progress in Latin America", Costa Rica holds the fourth best position in Latin America regarding the quality of its institutional environment. This index summarizes the opinions of business communities as to the rule of law and control of corruption. This ranking puts Costa Rica within the world average.

Costa Rica is one of a few Latin American countries where a legal body, jurisprudence and doctrine in administrative law has developed. In Costa Rica the time for the judgment on a particular case in administrative proceedings depends on the nature of the proceedings, the complexity of the matter, and the administrative authority before which it is being processed. Article 261 of the General Law For Public Administration provides that the maximum duration term of an ordinary administrative procedure is of two months; however, this type of proceedings normally take between six months and one year in average.

With respect to the terms established for obtaining the response on requests, Article 331 of the General Law for Public Administration establishes a one-month term, after which, in absence of an answer on behalf of the Administration, it is understood that the request, license or permit in question was approved by positive silence.

Article 18 of the Law on Alternative Resolution of Conflicts and Promotion of Social Peace (Law 7727) establishes that the Government can submit a controversy with subjects of private law, such as corporations, to arbitration. However, jurisprudence as to the specific kinds of matters subject to this special jurisdiction has been quite restrictive.

In case of an administrative/executive action, an administrative dispute can be resolved within an average term of six months to one year, in accordance with its complexity. In case the matter is referred to the knowledge of the court of appeals or "casación", the final resolution of the case might take an estimate of four to five years. There is not a special court in charge of the resolution of disputes in matters related to foreign investment. The regulatory scheme for foreign investment is contemplated by several laws and regulations, and the solution of eventual conflicts shall be carried out through regular courts and proceedings.

In 1989, Article 10 of the Political Constitution was amended, with the purpose of creating the Constitutional Court of the Supreme Court of Justice, which essentially hears and resolves cases related to the protection of the individual fundamental rights.

Pursuant to Article 7 of the Costa Rican Constitution, the stipulations contemplated in international treaties have a hierarchical supremacy over internal laws and regulations. The Constitutional Court has also held that if there are international provisions regulating the fundamental rights of individuals in a more complete manner than the Constitution, the former apply. Furthermore, under the country's constitution, private parties can directly invoke international agreements as applicable law in domestic courts.

As far as corporate governance is concerned, Costa Rica is one of the few Latin American countries with a competition policy legislation. The "Ley de Promoción de la Competencia y Defensa Efectiva del Consumidor", No. 7472, dated

December 20th, 1994, was published in the Official Journal La Gaceta on January 19th, 1995. The *"Reglamento a la Ley de Promoción de la Competencia y Defensa Efectiva del Consumidor"* was adopted by Executive Decree No. 25234 MEIC of January 25, 1996 and published in the Official Journal La Gaceta on July 1st, 1996.

According to Article 18 of the aforementioned law, it is the Commission for the Promotion of Competition the specialized agency in charge of implementing and verifying the compliance with the competition policy legislation. The Commission is advices by *the Technical Unit of the Commission,* which has 12 employees, 9 of which are professionals in the areas of law and economics. The other 3 professionals considered as personnel support. For the conduction of certain studies, the Technical Unit may request the support of the Unit of Economic Studies of the Ministry of Economy, which has 10 professionals.

The Commission is part of the Ministry of Economy, however being a body with maximum legal de-concentration, the Commission is not accountable to the Minister, and constitutes itself the highest hierarchy in the administration for competition policy matters.

By comparison with legislation of industrial countries, Costa Rican legislation on competition policy is less repressive. According to Article 25 of the law, the maximum fine applicable is equal to six hundred and eighty times the lowest minimum monthly wage. However, when the Commission finds that the fault incurred is particularly serious, it can raise the fine up the higher amount between 10% of the annual sales obtained by the offender during the previous fiscal year or to 10% of the value of the assets property of the offender. Articles 16 (Mergers and Acquisitions) and 24, paragraphs c) and e), the existing legislation on competition allows the Commission to conduct only after merger controls.

## 2.5. Trade regime

In Costa Rica the main responsibility for trade policy implementation remains with the Ministry of Foreign Trade (COMEX). Over the last twenty years, Costa Rica has followed a trade policy meant to integrate its economy into international markets.[27] The implementation of this policy is reflected largely in the increase in Costa Rica's exports, the diversification of its products and markets, the increase in foreign direct investment, and the generation of employment by the export sector.

Three decades ago, Costa Rica was significantly dependent on four traditional agricultural goods (coffee, bananas, sugar and beef). Today, the country exports approximately 3 000 products. The number of agricultural goods sold abroad, such as watermelons, pineapples, melons, tubers and ornamental plants, has increased. In addition, Costa Rica is exporting high-technology products, such as computers, medicines, and medical equipment. As a result, the four traditional products accounted for only 14.3% of Costa Rica's total exports for the nine-month period ended September 30, 2002.

Costa Rica has also increased its market diversification during the last decade. Costa Rica exports are directed to approximately 130 different destinations around the world. Approximately 53.0% of Costa Rica's exports are sent to the United States, 16.5% to the European Union, 13.1% to Central America, 5.5% to Asia, and 2.9% and 2.1% are directed to countries in the Caribbean and South America, respectively.

Costa Rica's trade policy has three different but convergent dimensions: the domestic, multilateral and regional.

*On the domestic front, access for imported goods into Costa Rica's market has improved during the last seven years. Between 1995 and 2000, the average MFN tariff decreased from almost 12% to 7%. At 15% and 6%, average tariffs are considerably higher for agricultural than industrial products. As part of its market access commitments under the WTO Agreement on Agriculture, Costa Rica established tariff quotas for various agricultural products, (e.g. certain dairy and poultry products), although in almost all cases the filling levels have been low. Tariff reductions under preferential agreements have also contributed to greater access to Costa Rica's market.*

Costa Rica bound all but five tariff lines at the WTO, most at a maximum *ad valorem* rate of 45%; exceptions include mostly agricultural products, for which bound rates are in some cases as high as 233%. Closing the wide margin between applied and bound rates would further increase the predictability of market access conditions.

Imports are subject to domestic taxes applied uniformly with respect to their origin and in accordance with the national treatment principle, except for a few beverages. In addition, the domestic commercialization regime for alcoholic beverages discriminates between most imported and domestic products.

The use of non-tariff trade barriers appears limited. Costa Rica maintains various import restrictions and prohibition, generally for health, security or environmental reasons. No anti-dumping or countervailing duties were applied between 1995 and 2000, although four anti-dumping investigations were initiated. Likewise, with the exception of special safeguard measures applied to rice and beans under the WTO Agreement on Agriculture, no safeguard measures were taken.

There are no estimates of the global impact of programs to promote production and exports, although their number and diversity raise questions about their effectiveness and the economic distortions they might induce. To promote exports, Costa Rica maintains various special import regimes, notably the free zone regime. Export subsidies granted through a tax credit mechanism (Certificados de Abono Tributarios) were eliminated in late 1999 although some benefits are still being paid.

As at early 2001, Costa Rica maintained a tax on banana exports; taxes on coffee and meat exports were eliminated in 1999. From May 2000, Costa Rica has applied quantitative restrictions to coffee exports, retaining 20% of its export supply. The European Union grants Costa Rica's banana exports preferential market access through tariff quotas. Canada and the United States apply import quotas to its textile and apparel exports under the WTO Agreement on Textiles and Clothing.

Competition legislation adopted in the mid 1990s has resulted in an increasing number of actions by the competition authorities. However, competition remains restricted in a few but important areas. For instance, in practice the external and internal commercialization of domestically produced sugar is controlled by a cartel. Likewise, the State holds a monopoly on the importation, refining and wholesale distribution of crude oil, fuels derived from oil, asphalt and naphtha. The State also regulates the price of several goods and services, including public services and the marketing of various agricultural products such as bananas, coffee and sugar.

During the last seven years, Costa Rica has promoted the expansion of export-oriented manufactures through special fiscal regimes, notably of electronics under the free zone regime. However, despite efforts to generate linkages between export-oriented activities and the rest of the domestic industry, spillovers have so far been limited. Moreover, fostering those activities disadvantages other industries not enjoying the same privileges. Apart from the special fiscal regimes, measures to promote industrial production have focused on small and medium size enterprises.

In spite of its decreasing share in GDP, agriculture remains an important sector because of its contribution to employment and export earnings. A small number of agricultural products for domestic consumption are protected through higher than average tariffs and safeguard measures. Agricultural production in general benefits from other support measures, including fiscal incentives and specific financing programmes. Notwithstanding such support, and in spite of the traditionally high productivity of Costa Rica's producers, its two major agricultural exports, banana and coffee, have come under considerable pressure in recent years. This reflects both adverse international market conditions as well as competition for factors of production, particularly land and labour, from other sectors.

No major changes affected the services sector between 1995 and 2000. Tourism remains a main magnet for foreign exchange and investment, but long-standing inefficiencies in some other service areas impose unnecessary costs on other activities. The State retains monopoly rights on insurance, telecommunications and energy distribution.

OECD INVESTMENT POLICY REVIEWS – ISBN 92-64-10509-3 – © OECD 2004

Notwithstanding growing private participation in the banking industry, state-owned banks, favored by current regulations, still dominate the industry. Faced with vocal opposition from interest groups, the Government was unable to pass legislation it considered of prime importance to modernize key service activities, notably telecommunications. Pressure for reform arises from the widening gap between decades-old legislation, changing technology and new market imperatives. Pressure for reform arises from the widening gap between decades-old legislation, changing technology and new market imperatives.

In the external front, Costa Rica has followed a "double track" liberalization strategy leading to new commitments at a multilateral and regional level.

Since its accession to the GATT in 1990, Costa Rica has participated actively in the multilateral trading system. Costa Rica is a founding member of the WTO, and the Marrakesh Agreement Establishing the WTO has become an integral part of its domestic legislation. Costa Rica was also the first Latin American country in signing the Ministerial Declaration on Trade in Information Technology Products (ITA), and also has ratified the financial services protocol to the GATS. On the other hand, Costa Rica's commitments under the GATS are relatively limited; in general, for the sectors included in its Schedule, only market access and national treatment for consumption abroad have been bound.

Costa Rica has used the multilateral dispute settlement mechanism to protect its trade interests. Its decision to pursue a claim against certain measures affecting trade in underwear in the United States represented the first textile-related dispute ever brought to the WTO dispute settlement forum. This case – which was won by Costa Rica – represented a watershed in the evolution of the system and demonstrated the importance for small developing countries of having access to a rule-oriented international adjudication mechanism. In part due to this effect, both the authorities and the public at large hold a positive perception of the WTO and its impact on small countries. Recently, Costa Rica supported the launch of the Doha Development Round (the "Doha Development Round"), which is the current round of multilateral trade negotiations by and among the 144 countries that are members of the WTO.

The Agreement on Trade-related Aspects of Intellectual Property Rights (TRIPS Agreement) became part of Costa Rica's legislation through its ratification of the Marrakesh Agreement. Subsequently, Costa Rica has enacted or amended related domestic regulations to harmonize them with its international obligations and thus facilitate their application. Those changes were notified to the Council for Trade-Related Aspects of Intellectual Property Rights in late 2000.

At a regional level, since 1994, Costa Rica has been an active participant in the efforts to establish the Free Trade Area of the Americas (the "FTAA") and remains committed to the establishment of the FTAA by 2005. Costa Rica has supported new negotiation initiatives and currently chairs the Government Procurement Negotiating Group, the goal of which is to increase market access to North America, Latin America and South America.

Currently, Costa Rica has bilateral agreements in force with Mexico, the Dominican Republic, Chile, and Canada, and is in the process of negotiating free trade agreements with Panama and several Caribbean countries. Furthermore, the Central American countries, including Costa Rica, recently began negotiating a free trade agreement with the United States, Costa Rica's main trading partner, which is expected to improve Costa Rica's ability to attract foreign investment and help Costa Rica pursue and consolidate economic reforms.

Since the free trade agreement with Mexico was entered into in 1995, Costa Rican exports to Mexico have increased more than 500.0%, while Mexican imports into Costa Rica have tripled. Beginning in 1998, Costa Rica has replaced Guatemala as the main Central American supplier to the Mexican market. Similarly, Mexico has become the second largest exporter of goods to Costa Rica, after the United States.

The free trade agreement with the Dominican Republic became effective in 2002. Costa Rican exports to the Dominican Republic increased approximately 38.0% during the first 10 months of 2002, compared to the same period in 2001.

The free trade agreement between Costa Rica and Canada, which became effective in November 2002, represents the first agreement signed by a smaller country and a G-7 country. Market access provisions in the agreement grant certain Costa Rican products, most notably refined sugar and textiles, preferential access to the Canadian market.

The foreign trade sector depends largely on the economies of the other Central American countries as well as the economies of the United States and the European Union. Together, Costa Rica exports approximately 82.6% of its export products to these areas. The economic slowdown in those countries, together with the uncertainty regarding the magnitude, duration and impact of the economic slowdown on the world's economic growth, are important causes for the slowdown in demand for the Republic's exports and therefore the slowdown of the Republic's production of goods for export.

The United States of America is Costa Rica's most important trading partner. For the nine month period ended September 30, 2002, trade with the United States accounted for approximately US$599.0 million, or 15.3% of total exports, and approximately US$1 161.0 million, or 21.6% of total imports. These figures do not include exports from Free Zones, which, if added, would increase the amounts to 49.2%; imports from Free Zones to 54.2%.

Trade with members of the CACM has increased over the past five years as the economies of these countries have become more stable. Exports to CACM countries increased to US$388.5 million during the first nine months of

September 2002 from US$354.9 million for the same period in 1998. Imports from CACM countries remained constant at US$228.8 million for the first nine months of 2002 when compared with the same period in 1998. In the first nine months of 2002, Costa Rica maintained a positive trade balance with each member of the CACM.

The devaluation of the Mexican peso in December 1994, together with a free trade agreement with Mexico that became effective January 1, 1995, led to a significant increase of Costa Rican imports from Mexico during 1995 and 1996. Imports from Mexico continued to increase in 1998, 1999 and 2000 at approximately the same pace as imports generally. However, imports from Mexico decreased by 2.6% in 2001 and 4.1% in the nine-month period ended September 30, 2002. Following the enactment of the bilateral free trade agreement, Costa Rica's exports to Mexico increased significantly in 1996 and continued to grow in 1997. Costa Rica's exports to Mexico declined sharply in 1998, grew at the same pace as exports generally in 1999, decreased by 6.6% in 2000, and decreased by 30.8% in 2001 from its level in 2000.

During the first nine months of 2002, exports to Mexico represented 1.2% of total exports, a proportion that has been generally maintained since 1998; while imports for the same period represented 4.8% of total imports. In previous years, this percentage has remained between 5% and 6% of total imports.

## 2.6. Investment regime

In Costa Rica there is not any registration requirement for FDI, nor is any FDI project subject to screening or approval. Furthermore in Costa Rica there is not any specific legislation targeted exclusively foreign investment and there are not specific limitations applicable to foreign investments.

According to the jurisprudence of the Constitutional Tribunal established in 1989, by constitutional mandate, foreigners and nationals are considered equal and are granted the same rights and obligations. However, given that such constitutional mandate has been effectively implemented by jurisprudence, existing legislation discriminating against foreign investment may remain applicable until an citizen challenges such discrimination through a writ of "amparo", a special but informal and relatively fast procedure to safeguard basic civil rights.

For those sectors in which limitations to private participation exist, the same rules are applied both to nationals and foreigners. However, there sectors closed to domestic as well as foreign investment by public or publicly authorized private monopolies. They are the following:

● Coal deposits, oil sources and reserves, and any other hydrocarbon substances, as well as radioactive mineral deposits existing in the national territory and its seabed; mineral resources existing in the national territory and its seabed, regardless of the kind, physical state and nature of the substances that they content.

- Ownership of railways, naval ports and airports (their administration may be granted under concession).
- Import, refinery, distribution and wholesale distribution of crude oil, derived fuels, asphalt and naphtha.
- Alcohol production.
- Postal communication services.
- Cable and wireless services.
- Energy exploitation (forces that may be obtained from the waters of public dominion in the national territory).
- Water supply services; collect and disposal of sewage water and liquid industrial waste; aqueduct and sewage system services.
- Insurance and reinsurance.

In Costa Rica there are no different corporate tax rates applicable depending on the nationality of the corporation, nor there are any special incentives or allowances applicable to foreign-owned firms. However, in the country there are other special incentives or allowances applicable to all corporations depending on participation on a special scheme. Given that most export-oriented FDI in Costa Rica locate in FTZs, it is worth explaining in greater detail what is entailed by this particular regime.

The **Free Zone Regime** ruled by law No. 7210 of November 23, 1990 encompasses a number of benefits and incentives granted by the Government to those companies that make new investments in the country. It applies not only to export processing industries but also to commercial enterprises, service companies, industrial parks managerial companies, research entities and companies operating shipyards and docks to build or repair ships.

Under this regime, companies are allowed to enjoy the following incentives for a certain period:

- 100% exemption from import duties and consular taxes on raw materials, parts and components.
- 100% exemption from import duties and consular taxes on fuels, oils and lubricants not locally produced.
- 100% exemption from import duties and consular taxes on machinery, equipment and certain vehicles.
- 100% exemption from sales and consumption taxes on local purchases of goods and services.

- 100% exemption from taxes on profits, dividends, etc., for a period of 8 (12) years and a 50% exemption for the following 4 (6) years for enterprises in more developed areas (lesser developed areas).
- 100% exemption from municipal taxes for 10 years (in certain areas).
- 100% exemption from taxes on profit remittances abroad.
- Tax credit equivalent to 10% of salaries paid by enterprises in lesser developed areas.
- Other non-fiscal benefits.

The investment regime applicable to foreign investment in Costa Rica has also been complemented by a series of bilateral investment treaties (BITs) negotiated by the government, the majority of which have been negotiated during the last decade. As most countries of the continent, Costa Rica has negotiated BITs which grant the right of establishment to most FDI – that is the case of the BIT with negotiated with Canada – as well as BITs which, following the European model, contain admission clauses. Table 2.7 lists all the BITs negotiated by Costa Rica up to date as well those which are in process of negotiation. In addition to the BITs, Costa Rica has also negotiated Free Trade Agreements (FTAs) which contain investment chapters. That is the case of the FTAs with Mexico and Dominican Republic.

Table 2.7. **Costa Rica bilateral investment treaties (BITs)**

| BITs in force | Concluded negotiations | Ongoing negotiations |
| --- | --- | --- |
| Argentina | Ecuador | Austria |
| Canada | Finland | Barbados |
| Chile | Bolivia | Brazil |
| China (Taiwan) | Poland | Denmark |
| Czech Republic | | Greece |
| France | | Ireland |
| Germany | | Jamaica |
| Great Britain | | Italy |
| Korea | | Norway |
| Netherlands | | Peru |
| Paraguay | | Portugal |
| Spain | | Rumania |
| Switzerland | | Sweden |
| Venezuela | | Uruguay |

Source: COMEX.

## 2.7. Investment Promotion Agency: Costa Rican Investment Board (CINDE)

Founded in 1982 with significant involvement of the Costa Rican private sector, and with substantial funding from the United States Agency for International Development (USAID), the Costa Rica Investment Board (CINDE) is a private, apolitical, non-profit organisation whose mission is, on the one hand, to attract foreign direct investment in specific sectors of the economy; and on the other, to advocate for changes and constant improvement in the investment climate so as to increase the country's attractiveness for the performance of certain economic activities where Costa Rica enjoys a competitive position. In view of the importance of its role, CINDE was declared of public interest by the Costa Rican government in 1984.

It is undeniable that the influx of foreign investment is of the utmost importance to Costa Rica, not only for balance of payment reasons, but most importantly as a significant contributor to the generation of employment, technology transfer and diversification of exports. Such recognition is reflected on the direct relationship established, more consistently since early 90's, between the national development strategy, the FDI policy and the developmental impact. It can be clearly observed that Costa Rica's success stems from the design and implementation of a developmental policy aimed at using FDI to resolve a developmental challenge. It was precisely the adoption of a strategy that focused on more sophisticated assembly activities, the use of highly skilled human resources and on a more targeted approach to attracting FDI that enabled Costa Rica to attract some of the most important high tech and services companies worldwide, i.e. Intel, Abbott Laboratories and Procter and Gamble.

As a rule, foreigners have exactly the same rights as locals for conducting business in Costa Rica. Therefore, companies and individuals can establish operations in several ways and in almost every industry without limitations. This also means that the possibility of creating strategic alliances between foreign and local companies is only limited by the ability to identify the appropriate market opportunity and finding the right local partner.

Within that context, CINDE works to foster Costa Rica's development, by serving as a catalyst and facilitator for the investment process in the country. Its non-political stance, coupled with its broad-based interest position, allow CINDE to maintain excellent relations with both the public and the private sectors. More than that, given that CINDE's performance and chances to succeed are closely linked to the quality of "the product" it has to offer and how effectively it portrays Costa Rica as an ideal investment location, a continued and renewed improvement of the country's investment climate becomes key to adequately carry out this task. Therefore, although it goes

OECD INVESTMENT POLICY REVIEWS – ISBN 92-64-10509-3 – © OECD 2004

beyond CINDE's scope of direct activity to actually materialize those changes needed to raise national competitiveness, the role the agency plays in highlighting issues and putting pressure upon the system to try to provoke those necessary modifications to the prevailing business environment is crucial. It should be borne in mind that CINDE enjoys a privileged insight and position that allows the agency to learn first hand about the main concerns of the investors, to fully understand the obstacles they face while operating in the country and even the reasons why certain projects decided in favor of another country. In consequence, CINDE's assessment and policy recommendations are valuable tools to establish national priorities in terms of education, availability of human resources with certain skills, infrastructure, availability of certain services at competitive costs, etc.

CINDE is organized to promote Costa Rica as a competitive investment site in three sectors that benefit from significant strengths and advantages that the country offers: Medical Devices, Electronics, and Services. A fourth sector, Special Projects, includes projects in areas such as textiles, tourism, and others.

Investment promotion executives support the work in each sector and specialized researchers analyze specific market segments and tendencies, identify sub sectors of interest, study and generate relevant information and lists of potential investors.

CINDE's offices in New York and California proactively look for companies interested in expanding operations abroad and provide tailor-made services to investors. An additional team in Costa Rica advises on how to do business in the country, creates custom itineraries according to the investor's needs, and provides support during and after the establishment of operations. CINDE develops long-term relationships with those investors established in the country and is committed to provide them with continued assistance as may be required. It is not by coincidence that the most recent World Investment Report 2002 published by the United Nations Conference on Trade and Development (UNCTAD) distinguished CINDE as "a state-of-the-art IPA".

ISBN 92-64-10509-3
OECD Investment Policy Reviews
Caribbean Rim: Costa Rica, Dominican Republic and Jamaica
© OECD 2004

# Chapter 3

# Investor Perceptions and Policy Recommendations

## 3.1. Investor perceptions[28]

"My niche is not low cost, my niche is quality". This is a statement of a foreign investor who opted to locate a suit factory in Costa Rica less than five years ago, and to a great extent, reflects the perception that most international investors have of the country as a location to do business. Indeed, due to numerous factors, among others its social security and salary structure, Costa Rica's comparative advantage to attract FDI is far from relying on low-cost wages. In fact, relative to other countries of the region, average wages in Costa Rica are significantly higher. However, despite this fact, as this report has demonstrated, during the last decade Costa Rica has managed to be a success story as far as FDI attraction is concerned.

Foreign investors may not perceive Costa Rica as a cheap place to do business, however, they perceive the country as a place where – due to several reasons – FDI can be instrumental for foreign firms to remain competitive in international markets. In this regard, four main variables seem to be key for foreign investors:

● Political stability and rule of law.

● Productivity, education and culture of the workforce.

● Geography.

● Preferential access to US market.

Foreign investors perceive Costa Rica as a stable country, not only from a political point of view, but also from a social perspective. The risk of armed conflict or social unrest is perceived as minimal. This view seem to stem from the fact that Costa Rica unilaterally abolished its armed forces half a century ago, and has the longest tradition of continuous democratic rule in Latin America. The political stability of the country is also associated to the development of a relatively expanded socioeconomic middle class, which has enabled the Costa Rican society to avoid the social polarization existing in other Latin American countries. These factors have contributed to the relatively calm political and socioeconomic environment the country enjoys today, a fact which has accurately being perceived by foreign investors.

Political stability is also associated with the strong rule of law and political transparency foreign investors perceive as existing in Costa Rica. Indeed, contrary to other countries of the region, corruption is not perceived as a problem to do business in Costa Rica. Further, although not perceived as particularly expedite, the judicial system is perceived as fair and impartial. The role of a free press as a tool to ensure political transparency and attempt to control any kind of power abuse is also recognized by foreign investors. Most major economic, social or political issue is subject to an open national debate through the mass media, allowing the different sectors of the society to identify where the interests of the different pressure groups lie.

Productivity, education and culture of the workforce are other variables foreign investors perceive as key factors leading them to locate their investments in Costa Rica. Indeed, given the higher cost structure existing in the country, the quality of the labor force is perceived as pivotal for the competitiveness of foreign business located in the Costa Rica. The high educational level is valued not only because it is an asset in itself,[29] but also because a skilled workforce is also able to learn other productive techniques more rapidly, making it more flexible and able to cope with the continuous productive changes generated by technological progress. Learning capacity is key for FDI projects entailing highly sophisticated productive processes, which often require additional specialized training for those employed in the project. Foreign investors in Costa Rica perceive the local workforce as productive and able, to such degree that those qualities offset the higher cost such labor force entail. However, foreign investors are also beginning to perceive Costa Rican workforce as numerically limited. In some sectors, foreign investors are planning significant expansion of operations and have expressed concern that the existing professional supply may not be sufficient to satisfy their demand in the near future. This is particularly true in sectors requiring sophisticated English proficiency and computer skills. Improving mass education in these two areas is then one of the objectives Costa Rican investment policy should pursue in the short term.

Geography is perceived by foreign investors as another variable which makes Costa Rica as an attractive location to invest. Geography is relevant from two perspectives. First, the country is centrally located, close to the United States – 2 and half hours flight time from Miami – and other potential export destinations. Second, the physical geography of the country, with its vast natural reserves, have also played a role in making top executives to like the living environment and favor Costa Rica as nice place to settle operations. The international reputation of the country as an environmentally friendly place also seems to add appeal to locate facilities in Costa Rica as the chances for having the investment projects being politically questioned on environmental concerns at the home base of the multinational tend to diminish.

Preferential access to the US market has also played a key role in the investors' perceptions of Costa Rica as an adequate place to locate their investments. Indeed, most foreign investors are from the United States, and have opted to invest in Costa Rica to remain competitive in the US market.

This fact explains to a great extent why this sector is embracing the initiative to negotiate the CAFTA (the US Central America Free Trade Agreement), as this treaty would lock in the market access conditions favoring their export-oriented investments in the country.

The perceptions of foreign investors as to the performance of the State in fostering an investment-friendly environment are mixed, although overall they tend to be positive. On the one hand, foreign investors have recognized that the national government has played a key role in attracting key FDI projects, and consider that the Costa Rican government understands the strategic importance FDI has for the development of the country. On the other, foreign investors perceive the performance of the State machinery as heterogeneous.

Infrastructure and administrative redtape when establishing the investment are aspects which foreign investors criticize, although they also recognize the efforts undertaken in the last four years to make the public administration more efficient and foster further private investment in the development of key infrastructure projects highly needed by the country. While the quality of the provision of some public services is ranked very positively among foreign investors, in particular health and education, the quality in the provision of other services, in particular, utilities such as electricity, telecommunication services and water supply receive a poorer evaluation. These are areas controlled by State monopolies, the reform of which have been subject to national debate for a couple of years. This is an area Costa Rica will need to seriously assess in order to maintain its competitiveness for FDI.

## 3.2. Conclusions and policy recommendations

Costa Rica represents a success story of a small developing economy attracting increasing flows of FDI. As demonstrated by this report, FDI inflows in Costa Rica not only have significantly grown during the last decade, but have also had a positive qualitative impact in the process of economic development of the country. This positive impact stems from the four main features of FDI in Costa Rica:

- green field investment;
- export-oriented;
- focused on the manufacturing; and
- services sectors.

Thus, FDI has meant not only increased foreign exchange, but also jobs in relatively higher paid sectors and a significant transfer of technology.

Thus, the pattern in the evolution of FDI inflows in Costa Rica during the last decade is clear, and can be explained in terms of several variables, both internal and external.

From an internal perspective, to a great extent it can be said that the Costa Rica is harvesting the results of decades of investment in its human development, in particular education. Further, Costa Rica is today benefiting from a continuous economic policy which has attempted to insert the Costa Rican economy to international markets. Indeed, despite that government administrations have changed every four years, since 1982, all the administrations have opted to maintain the basic market-oriented economic policy. This macroeconomic policy continuity has enabled the country to begin to rip the benefits of the new development model. However, the reform process has not been completed yet. Compared to other Latin American countries, the pace of economic reform has been slower. This is particularly true in the services sector, where key areas still remain in the hands of State monopolies, and the reform of which is still subject to debate among the different segments of the Costa Rican civil society.

From an external perspective, the role of the CBI in enabling Costa Rica to attract increasing FDI flows has been extremely important. Indeed, as this report clearly shows, most export-oriented FDI is geared to the US market. This pattern reveals that important US based corporations have understood the importance of using FDI in Costa Rica as an effective means to safeguard and expand their market share in the United States and in other international markets. The success of this strategy has been, then, to position Costa Rica within a vertical integration productive strategy of both US and non-US multinationals. Nevertheless, the success of Costa Rica in attracting high tech FDI flows has yet to be complemented by linking the domestic productive sector to the former. Indeed, the Costa Rican productive sector is basically comprised by micro and small enterprises (MSEs). Despite some initial success stories, the linkages between these MSEs and the international corporations based in the country so far has been limited, and further work is required in this particular area to ensure that the benefits of FDI in the local economy are maximized.

The significantly positive results in terms of Costa Rica's export expansion and diversification clearly suggests the path that Costa Rican investment policy should follow in the future. Costa Rican policy makers understand that the future of the development of the country lies, to a great extent, in two main objectives: to position the country in international markets, and to link its domestic productive apparatus to the dynamic international corporations based in the country, developing and strengthening the "clusterisation" concept and strategy. Therefore, investment policy should be targeted to deal with those two fronts: the external and the internal.

On the external side, Costa Rica urgently needs to lock in its preferential access to foreign markets, in particular the United States. This policy objective entails to pursue an active trade policy in multilateral and regional fora. In this particular front, the Costa Rican government has done its homework. The negotiation of CAFTA will definitively represent a watershed in Costa Rica's investment policy. CAFTA will enable Costa Rica not only to lock in its preferential market access conditions to the United States, but also, CAFTA will be instrumental in better positioning the country in the minds of international investors. Smaller economies like Costa Rica, which lack a broad and attractive domestic market to lure FDI, are more dependent on signaling mechanisms to lure FDI. In this regard, the negotiation of CAFTA will be a key signal to US investors that Costa Rica is an attractive and safe place to invest. Thus, on this particular respect, the main challenge Costa Rica should face in the near future is to use the momentum generated by the CAFTA negotiations to position the country in the international investment community.

On the internal side, as this report clearly demonstrate, to a great extent, Costa Rican policy makers have very different worries about a series of domestic problems that affect other countries of the region. Costa Rica can profit from political stability, strong and transparent institutions, a strong rule of law and a productive, flexible and educated workforce. However, despite the significant achievements in these fronts, Costa Rica still has to find efficient means to consolidate them and undertake a qualitative leap in its process of economic development. This report demonstrates that the Costa Rican investment policy should focus on at least three main goals:

- promoting the modernization of the country's infrastructure;
- continuing improving the education of its human capital; and
- fostering backward linkages between FDI and domestic SMEs.

Since the debt crisis at the beginning of the 1980s, due to fiscal constraints, the capacity of the government to pursue and finance public works has decreased significantly. In a country where significant parts of the physical infrastructure supporting the productive sector remains in the hands of the State, the contraction in public investment meant almost a complete paralysis in infrastructure development for more than a decade.

In Costa Rica, public works projects are urgently needed to increase the competitiveness of the productive sectors and to facilitate the attraction of investment and new technology. Given the tight budget constraints to finance public investment in the country:

- promotion of public work concessions has been identified as the means by which these urgent needs can be satisfied;
- thus, the identification of mechanisms to enable this system of adjudication of public contracts to operate efficiently ranks among the most urgent needs the country currently faces in the field of infrastructure development.

This report has recognized the significant development accomplished by Costa Rica in the field of education. Despite having literacy rates comparable to industrial economies, Costa Rica needs to:

- reassess the role of education in the fostering the competitiveness of the country in an increasingly competitive world.

Thus, another area where Costa Rica should devote attention in order to promote further systemic competitiveness of its economy is the field of mass education and strengthening the training of its current and future labor force. Given the particular characteristics of FDI inflows in Costa Rica, the country should:

- reassess its concept of literacy in order to include two urgently needed elements: English proficiency and computer literacy.

To provide the majority of the population with these basic skills has become increasingly important, not only as a means to promote better opportunities for all the inhabitants of the country, but also to ensure the competitiveness of the Costa Rican economy as a whole.

Promotion of backward linkages between FDI and domestic MSEs is the third area on which investment policy in Costa Rica should focus. Despite comprising 62% of the total number of exporting enterprises in the country, in 1999 participation of MSEs in Costa Rica's total exports represented only 13% of the total value. Within this context, there is a need to:

- implement effective mechanisms to internationalize Costa Rican MSEs, attempting to enable these enterprises to participate from the benefits of free trade and to compete in international markets.

The three areas mentioned above could be taken into consideration for an investment policy reform agenda in the context of the CRII.

# Notes

1. *Source:* Central Bank of Costa Rica.

2. The relative weight of Spain among Costa Rica's main sources of FDI is underestimated in this table. In fact, Spain's share of FDI inflows in Costa Rica is very likely to be much higher than the 0.8 per cent indicated by the table. This misrepresentation stems from the fact that the data corresponding to 1995 and 1996 FDI inflows does not include the tourism sector, which was measured separately. For 1995 FDI in tourism reached US$66.9 million and for 1996 US$53.6 million. As most Spanish investments in Costa Rica are concentrated in this sector, Spain may in fact represent the third or fourth source of FDI in the country.

3. These firms are: AES, Enron, Coastal, Seaboard, and Union Fenosa. TRICOM, in which Motorola has a stake, ranks 15th. It is the second largest provider of long distance and cellular phone services in the country.

4. As a matter of fact, contrary to most Latin American countries, Costa Rica has never enacted foreign investment law, nor established any screening mechanism or even FDI registry.

5. Indeed, during the 1990s, Costa Rican exports multiplied by a factor of five, passing from US$1 676 million in 1990 to US$6 719 million in 1999. This point is further developed in Section 2.3 below.

6. This point is developed in Section 2.3 below.

7. Any discussion involving the reality of small and medium enterprises (SMEs) must start by clarifying the parameters used to consider a particular business as part of this business category. The criteria used for this purpose vary significantly, not only between countries, but also among different institutions in the same country. The chart below illustrates that different definitions used by diverse institutions in Costa Rica. One criticism against the use of this criteria has been that the definition of SMEs must be more dynamic and not be restricted to the number of employees or volume of sales, specially in the context of a dynamic and open economy, where exports can fluctuate and where the criteria used by other countries should also be taken into consideration. Thus, Broadly speaking, in Costa Rica a micro-enterprise tends to comprise less than 15 employees, a small

OECD INVESTMENT POLICY REVIEWS – ISBN 92-64-10509-3 – © OECD 2004

enterprise tends to comprise around 50 employees and a medium enterprise less than 1 000 employees.

| PRONAPYME[1] | CABEI[2] | CRIC[3] | CCSS[4] |
|---|---|---|---|
| Micro-enterprise 1-9 employees | Micro-enterprise 1-5 employees | Micro-enterprise 1-5 employees | Range-based classification |
| Small enterprise 10-20 employees | Small enterprise 6-40 employees | Small enterprise 6-20 employees | 1-4 employees |
| | | | 5-9 employees |
| | | Medium enterprise 21-100 employees | 10-19 employees |
| | | | 20-99 employees |

1. PRONAPYME: Programa nacional para la pequeña y mediana empresa, Program for SMEs.
2. CABEI: Central American Bank of Economic Integration.
3. CRIC: Costa Rican Industrial Chamber.
4. CCSS: Caja Costarricense del Seguro Social, Social Healthcare Institute.
*Source:* OECD.

8. Source: Caja Costarricense del Seguro Social (CCSS).

9. Source: Fundacion para el Desarrollo Sostenible (FUNDES).

10. Source: Instituto Nacional de Estadística y Censo (INEC).

11. Source: PROCOMER.

12. An exception of the predominant trend in the export behaviour of most SMEs is the software sector, where business with few employees and initial capital have been able to become true "small multinational enterprises" operating in several countries, even beyond the Americas.

13. In 2002, preliminary estimations indicate that total GDP will increase to US$16 886.5 million, leading to a per capita GDP of US$4 102.3. Source: Central Bank of Costa Rica.

14. Based on preliminary data, the fastest growing sectors of the Costa Rican economy in 2002 were transportation; financial intermediation and insurance, warehousing and telecommunications (which includes cellular phone services); and electricity and water. Source: Central Bank of Costa Rica.

15. Source: Central Bank of Costa Rica.

16. These projects include the US$105.0 million investment by Four Seasons Hotels and Resorts in the Papagayo's tourist region, the US$38.0 million, 350 room expansion of Hotel Costa Smeralda, the inauguration of the US$21.0 million Alegro Papagayo Hotel, and the proposed US$10.0 million Hilton Airport Hotel. During 2000, investments in tourism projects totalled approximately US$204 million, compared with US$24.2 million during 1999.

17. Source: Central Bank of Costa Rica.

18. *Ibid.*

19. By Costa Rican Law, seaports, airports, railroads, sewage, water distribution, telecommunications and energy are State monopolies.

20. There is another international airport located in Liberia, Guanacaste, in the northwest part of the country, close to some of the most important beach tourist destinations. From Liberia major international airlines have begun international passenger services, linking that town with major cities in the United States and Canada.

21. Human Development Index, 2001.

22. National Integrated System for the Competitiveness of Technical Education (SINETEC), Technical Education and professional Formation in Costa Rica, 2001.

23. Source: July 2002 Annual Household Survey.

24. Nevertheless, based on information compiled by the Department of Labor Relations of the Ministry of Labor, in 2001, there were in Costa Rica 4 strikes, one in the public sector, which lasted 1 day, and three in the private sector, all of them related to banana sector. All three strikes lasted a total of 3 days.

25. Source: State of the Nation Statistical Compendium, October 2001.

26. Source: Labor Ministry, 2001; Costa Rica's Labor Code.

27. This policy has been quite successful. Indeed, between 1995 and 2000, trade in goods and services rose from some 78% to 97% as a proportion of GDP.

28. The conclusions included in this section are derived from several activities conducted by CINDE, the Costa Rican Investment Board, including bilateral discussions, roundtables and a business survey comprising the top 20 foreign investors in the country.

29. Indeed, the most important FDI projects in Costa Rica during the last decade have required the availability of a significant number of professionals in different areas such as informatics, engineering, business administration and other technical careers.

OECD INVESTMENT POLICY REVIEWS – ISBN 92-64-10509-3 – © OECD 2004

# Jamaica

Investor perceptions of Jamaica as a location for Foreign Direct Investment (FDI) have improved within the last decade and investors are generally supportive of the Jamaican government's efforts to attract FDI. Political stability and democratic government rank high among the factors drawing investors to Jamaica. This report looks at areas which need to be improved as well as concrete measures to be implemented by the government (often with the support of international organisations) to further enhance Jamaica's investment climate. Jamaica's main objective is to transform itself into a knowledge-based economy, using foreign private investment as a strategic tool to meet its development goals of human capital improvement, increased productivity, job creation, transfer of technology and export diversification.

# Preface

Over the past decade, the Jamaican economy has been adjusting to an increasingly competitive world. The Government of Jamaica has therefore embarked on a number of strategies geared towards preparing businesses for the dynamic global environment and enhancing the country's capacity to compete in the global marketplace. These include liberalising the trade and investment regimes to allow for greater integration in the global economy, as well as legislative and regulatory reforms.

To retain our position as a major recipient of Foreign Direct Investment (FDI) in the Caribbean region we recognize that the legislative and regulatory reform must provide increased transparency and enhance the efficacy and relevance of regulations related to taxation, trade facilitation, and other elements that will improve the investment climate. In this context your report is very timely as it provides the basis for evaluating our systems and processes through the comprehensive analysis of our investment regime. Our movement toward a global integrated economy will require strengthening the framework for private investment and initiatives and hence a more seamless government machinery must be developed.

I commend this effort as one which will aide our thrust to improve the business environment, enhance competitiveness and facilitate development.

Paul Robertson, PhD.
Minister of Development
Office of the Prime Minister

ISBN 92-64-10509-3
OECD Investment Policy Reviews
Caribbean Rim: Costa Rica, Dominican Republic and Jamaica
© OECD 2004

# Executive Summary

J amaica, the third largest island in the Caribbean, is a parliamentary democracy half the size of the state of Vermont. Known for being the birthplace of reggae and for its pristine beaches and densely forested Blue Mountains, it is home to 2.7 million people who had an income per capita of US$2 750 in 2001. The country experienced modest growth rates over the past three years (0.7 per cent in 2000, 1.7 per cent in 2001, and 0.6 per cent in 2002), having been beset by external and domestic shocks. Foreign direct investment (FDI), in contrast, increased sharply in recent years to reach a total of US$613.9 million in 2001, a nominal increase of 30 per cent compared to the previous year.

After struggling to achieve economic growth in the 1970s and during many years throughout the following decade, at the beginning of the 1990s Jamaica embarked on an economic program aimed at lowering inflation, removing exchange controls, and liberalizing trade. These reforms were accompanied by others, which eliminated barriers to investment and contributed to attract FDI.

Jamaica is essentially a services economy. Whereas agriculture accounted for 6.5 per cent of GDP in 2001, the services sector captured 63 per cent of the total during the same year. Tourism, information and communication technology (ICT) and telecommunications, chemicals and minerals, manufacturing, textiles, and culture (film and music) are the core sectors benefiting from FDI.

The Jamaican economic policy has played a significant role in improving the business environment for foreign investors, albeit more remains to be done to ensure that investors can reap the full benefits of their efforts. The country has been successful in reducing inflation from 50 per cent in 1991 to 7 per cent in 2002 but economic growth remains sluggish. The key economic challenges of the Government lie with the restoration of the fiscal account so as to induce a reduction in interest rates and spur demand, and the implementation of a monetary policy, which does not lead to an overvalued currency and higher interest rates, hence resulting in lower demand and income growth. In recent years, the country's exchange rate policy has had a dampening effect on the ability of Jamaican-based companies to export, albeit the Jamaican dollar began to weaken in 2002 given the pressures of the increasing fiscal deficit. The Government must also keep encouraging the recovery of the financial sector, which benefited from a rescue package from 1997 to 2002. Cognizant of all these factors, the Government requested a Staff-Monitored Program (SMP) with the International Monetary Fund and a World Bank's Country Assistance Strategy. As to the financial sector, the

Government is implementing a restructuring plan with a view to fostering competition among strong capitalized institutions.

FDI remains an integral part of the development strategy of the country. Jamaica's main objective is to transform itself into a knowledge-based economy generating value-added exports and sustaining wealth creation with high-paying jobs, using foreign private investment as a strategic tool to meet its development goals of human capital improvement, increased productivity, job creation, transfer of technology, and export diversification.

The Government is targeting the ICT sector (call centres and back-office centres, and software development services) to create employment and increase export earnings. In the tourism sector, the Government is promoting diversification focusing on attracting European investors (e.g. Spain), broadening its products to include eco-tourism, and heritage and wellness tourism, and encouraging local expansions through timeshare. In the non-services sector, investments for agribusiness (aquaculture/fresh produce), recycling, plastics and minerals/chemicals, as well as value-added products in food processing are the key priorities.

As a result of very generous incentive packages and other measures implemented over the last decade, the country continues to be very attractive for foreign investors. Numerous opportunities are now available with the liberalization of the telecom sector, completed in March 2003 when Cable and Wireless lost its monopoly on international communications. As mentioned above, other targeted sectors include the fast-growing tourism industry, the nascent but vibrant ICT sector, specialized minerals and the bauxite-rich mining industry, the agribusiness sector, and also the music and film industries.

The Government's economic program has aimed at strengthening the framework for private investment. Numerous initiatives have been implemented in this regard. For example, measures aimed at reducing the deficiencies in infrastructure services, particularly with respect to water shortages, inadequate sewage facilities, and the underdeveloped transport network have been prioritized. Additional investment requirements in the infrastructure sectors are estimated to amount to US$600 million in power and US$1 billion in the water sector over the next fifteen years, and the Government is actively encouraging the participation of the private sector.

In 2001, the Jamaica Public Service Co. (JPSCo.), the country's electricity and power company, was privatized and is now owned by US-based Mirant Corp. More recently, in March 2003, the Government announced that it plans to establish a new licensing regime in the next legislative year, under the new Water Supply and Sewerage Services Act, which will remove the power of granting licenses for water and sewerage projects from the National Water Commission (NWC). Prime Minister Patterson made this announcement at the ground-breaking ceremony for the US$39-million Great River/Lucea Water Supply System. The objective of the Government is to give the private sector a legitimate role in the water sector with the appropriate regulatory controls to ensure high quality service and fair tariffs. The Great River/Lucea Water Supply project, which is jointly funded by BNP-Paribas of France, and the National Commercial Bank (owned by Canadian-based AIC) and Pan Caribbean Financial Services of Jamaica, will also receive financing from the French pipe manufacturing firm, Pont-A-Mousson, and will benefit from the expertise of the contractors of the project, French-based SOGEA/SATOM. Moreover, in January 2003, the Government signed an agreement sub-contracting all the rights and responsibilities in respect of management, operation, maintenance and development of the Sangster International Airport in Montego Bay to Vancouver Airport Services for a period of thirty years. The consortium also includes Spanish construction and services group Dragados, Chilean group Agunsa, and Israeli-based construction company Ashtorm.

Over the last decade, Jamaica has implemented a major privatization program under which several public sector entities have been divested, though some 150 enterprises remain in the public sector. To ensure that the country takes full advantage of its privatization program, it is implementing a regulatory framework providing investor confidence, ensuring competition, and protecting consumer interests.

Other Government initiatives aimed at improving the investment and business climate in Jamaica includes the modernization of the Customs Department, under the *Public Sector Modernisation Programme (PSMP)*, scheduled to be completed in 2005. The Customs Department will be one of the revenue departments and as such it will fall under the *Tax Administration Reform Programme (TAXARP)*. All the revenue departments have been brought under one umbrella (TAXARP) to create the standardization of all processes and procedures. The objective is to achieve a faster and more efficient service to travellers and importers, enhance compliance from importers as well as to further the capacity to detect illegal imports. Moreover, in November 2002, the Inter-American Development Bank (IADB) approved a loan of US$17 million to help improve the country's access to Internet and e-government services. The funds will be used in part to help increase Internet access for 60 low-income communities throughout Jamaica. The resources will also be used to help upgrade Jamaica's e-government system. Businesses and citizens will be able to pay taxes online and obtain export and import permits on government Internet sites. The Government of Jamaica will administer the project, estimated at US$23 million, with remaining funds coming from local business contributions. In March 2003, the Government launched the *Corruption Prevention Commission*, which was established to detect, investigate and dispose of any acts of corruption among public servants. Under the Corruption

Prevention Act of 2000, a public servant is defined as any person who is employed in the public, municipal or parochial service in Jamaica, in the service of a statutory body or authority or a government company. Public servants earning in excess of J$ 2 million must submit their annual statutory declarations.

Several public-private sector initiatives are also playing a key role in creating a more enabling environment for business and private investment. The *New Economy Project (NEP)*, a US$6 million project funded by the United States Agency for International Development (USAID) since 2001, is aimed at improving the business environment for Jamaica's small, medium and micro enterprises, which dominate Jamaica's commercial landscape generating up to 40 per cent of GDP annually. These enterprises face significant constraints on their growth. These weaknesses include limited access to finance; weak financial management; and inadequate client management and marketing capacity, in particular with respect to developing linkages with foreign investors in the country. In February 2003, another project aimed at promoting private investment was launched. The *Jamaica's Cluster Competitiveness Project* is sponsored by the UK. Department for International Development (DFID), USAID, Jamaica's Ministry of Commerce, Science and Technology, and the Jamaica Exporters Association. The main objective of this two-year project is to mobilize eight clusters of firms to compete in the global marketplace. Also, in February 2003, the Government of Jamaica announced that it was spearheading legislation aimed at revising the incentive scheme regimes. The Government is working in collaboration with USAID and the Jamaica Chamber of Commerce on the *Jamaica Regulations Legislation and Process Improvement Project*. The intent is to look at the legislative framework, regulations and the administrative practices, which impinge on the efforts at ensuring that incentives are properly applied and effectively implemented. The Government however emphasized that any new incentive system has to be applied in a non-discriminatory manner to both local and foreign investors and allow for continuing assessment of the effectiveness of these incentive packages.

Investor perceptions of Jamaica as a prime location for FDI are improving. They are generally supportive of the Jamaican Government's efforts to attract FDI. Political stability and democratic Government rank high among the factors that draw investors to Jamaica. Investors also recognize that Jamaica's geographical proximity to North America, in particular easy air and shipping connections to Miami, good telecommunication services, and a qualified English-speaking workforce are major assets contributing to invite foreigners to invest in Jamaica. In the case of export-oriented investors, preferential market access to the United States under the Caribbean Basin Initiative (CBI) and the Caribbean Basin Trade Partnership Act (CBTPA), as well as to other Caribbean countries under the soon-to-be-fully-implemented CARICOM

Single Market and Economy are important considerations. Overall trade liberalization within the Free Trade Area of the Americas (FTAA) process will also provide foreign investors with additional market opportunities.

In a study conducted with twenty-nine existing or potential investors in Jamaica in August 1998, the US Department of Commerce highlighted three primary challenges identified by foreign investors.[1] The need to modernize infrastructure services topped the list of concerns, in particular, traffic congestion, poor urban and inter-city roads, and inadequate mass transit. The reliability of electricity and telecommunication services was also singled out. These two sectors have since then undergone major changes and benefited greatly from an influx of foreign direct investment, following the privatization and liberalization in each of these sectors, respectively. Crime and lack of security came second as challenges facing foreign investors. Personal safety as well as safety against pilferage were of particular concerns. Finally, labor issues were mentioned as having a negative impact on the overall investment climate. Traditionally, management-labor relations have been quite difficult in certain industries, as demonstrated by the number of strikes in recent years. However, the recommendations contained in the 1994 Labour Market Reform Committee report, which included modernizing the island's labor laws, implementing flexible work arrangements and restructuring the Ministry of Labour to make it better able to deal with industrial relations disputes, have yet to be fully implemented. The process of labor market reform is on going in the country. In January 2002, the National Labour Market Information System was launched as a tool to improve the flow of information to users on demand and supply side of the labor market.

Given its geographical proximity to North America and its English-speaking workforce, Jamaica offers numerous opportunities to investors but the country has yet to reap the full benefits of increased FDI, due in part to structural, regulatory, and macroeconomic constraints. Other factors also play a central role. Before the next plenary meeting of the Caribbean Rim Investment Initiative, a number of concrete measures should be implemented by the Government of Jamaica, with the support of international organisations such as the Inter-American Development Bank and the Organization for Economic Cooperation and Development (OECD), to improve the investment climate in the country. These measures should include:

a) the review of tax regulations to identify inefficiencies in statutes and procedures, and the strengthening of Jamaica's Double Taxation Treaty network, which does not include major investors such as France, Ireland, and Spain; and

b) the review of work permit procedures and business visas to facilitate greater access for key personnel related to investment projects.

Moreover, cognizant of the need to eliminate export subsidy programs such as free zones under the WTO Agreement on Subsidies and Countervailing Duties by the end of 2007, Jamaica should also carry out:

c) a review, as announced in February 2003, of its investment-related incentive packages, using a cost-benefit analysis to assess the use and provision of such incentives in the country.

With a view to encouraging linkages between foreign and local investors, Jamaica should undertake:

d) the establishment of a clearing house where small and medium-sized local companies meeting some well-defined standards of performance would register and could become suppliers of the foreign (and local) companies operating in free zones. Such a mechanism would encourage backward linkages; and

e) the establishment of an annual employment survey and assessment of economic inputs to monitor the progress in employment and linkages arising from FDI so as to use these results in shaping future policy.

Initiatives such as the recent IADB-financed e-government loan, which offers some 900 Jamaicans partial funding for high-level professional training in information and communication technology should be replicated and encouraged. As the country is targeting the ICT sector and telecommunications, Jamaica should review:

f) its investment in training and re-training programs aimed at improving the technological skills of its workforce with a view to increasing the competitive advantage of the country as a knowledge economy. In particular, Jamaica should undertake a full review of skills needed for the future and skills presently available so as to measure and address the gap with skills training, skills upgrading, and conversion programs.

Jamaica would also greatly benefit from:

g) the establishment of an annual benchmark survey of investors views on critical issues affecting investment decisions.

Reducing crime should remain one of the Government's top priorities, although it is worth noting that the real impact of violent crimes on FDI is difficult to assess since tourists and foreign business people are rarely the victims of such acts. Nevertheless, there is no doubt that it contributes to deter foreign investment. The Government is addressing this major problem and has recently adopted a multifaceted approach to strengthen and reorganize the police force and improve the country's access to the justice system.

ISBN 92-64-10509-3
OECD Investment Policy Reviews
Caribbean Rim: Costa Rica, Dominican Republic and Jamaica
© OECD 2004

# Chapter 1

# FDI Trends

## 1.1. Flows and stocks of FDI

FDI inflows into Jamaica grew at an average annual rate of 13.47 per cent from 1990 to 2000. The first half of the decade was marked by a succession of declines in FDI inflows and a negative average annual growth of 2.2 per cent (see Table 1.1). In contrast, the second half of the 1990s saw a steady increase in foreign direct investment flows into the country with an average growth rate reaching 29 per cent per year. A package of investment incentives provided by the Government of Jamaica (GOJ) in the key sectors of tourism, bauxite/alumina, agriculture, and manufacturing help explain the increase in FDI inflows during that period. Moreover, the GOJ allocated US$275 million for infrastructure projects in the tourist areas of the North Shore, whereas US$600 million were spent for the modernization and expansion of the mining sector in the late 1990s. Likewise, various investment programs were implemented to revitalize specific agricultural sectors such as sugar and bananas, as well as to assist apparel makers.

Table 1.1. **FDI inflows and outflows, 1990-2000**

Millions of US dollars

|  | 1990 | 1991 | 1992 | 1993 | 1994 | 1995 | 1996 | 1997 | 1998 | 1999 | 2000 |
|---|---|---|---|---|---|---|---|---|---|---|---|
| Inflows | 174.9 | 171.2 | 190.4 | 139.2 | 129.7 | 147.4 | 183.7 | 203.3 | 369.1 | 523.7 | 456.0 |
| Outflows | 37.0 | 38.0 | 48.0 | 61.3 | 52.7 | 66.3 | 93.3 | 56.6 | 82.0 | 94.9 | 74.3 |

Source: JAMPRO.

The improvement in the business climate, the adoption of a program aimed at privatizing state-owned enterprises, the consistent decline in the inflation rate for nearly a decade, and the proximity to the United States market are other variables that have played a central role in the increase of FDI inflows into Jamaica. Table 1.2 shows that Jamaica is among the top three largest recipients of FDI inflows in the Caribbean Basin, behind the Dominican Republic and Trinidad and Tobago in absolute terms. But Jamaica scores ahead of the Dominican Republic in FDI inflows per capita, having received US$227.37 in 2001 and $US181.15 in 2000, whereas the Dominican Republic attracted US$139.30 in 2001 and US$113.45 in 2000, respectively. Moreover, the increased flow to Jamaica in 2001 contrasts with what took place in several Latin American countries such as Argentina and Brazil, which experienced a significant reduction in FDI inflows in 2001.

**146**

Table 1.2. **FDI inflows in selected CARICOM and Central American countries**
Millions of US dollars

|  | 1998 | 1999 | 2000 | 2001 |
|---|---|---|---|---|
| Dominican Republic | 700 | 1 338 | 953 | 1 198 |
| Trinidad and Tobago | 730 | 643 | 662 | 835 |
| **Jamaica** | **369** | **524** | **471** | **613.9** |
| Panama | 1 296 | 652 | 603 | 513 |
| Guatemala | 673 | 155 | 230 | 456 |
| Costa Rica | 612 | 620 | 409 | 448 |
| El Salvador | 1 104 | 216 | 173 | 268 |
| Honduras | 99 | 237 | 282 | 195 |
| Nicaragua | 184 | 300 | 265 | 132 |
| St. Kitts and Nevis | 32 | 58 | 96 | 83 |
| Guyana | 47 | 48 | 67 | 56 |
| Antigua and Barbuda | 27 | 37 | 33 | 54 |
| Saint Lucia | 83 | 83 | 49 | 51 |
| Grenada | 49 | 42 | 36 | 34 |
| Belize | 16 | 17 | 19 | 18 |
| Haiti | 11 | 30 | 13 | 3 |

Source: UNCTAD, World Investment Report 2002. Geneva: UNCTAD, 2002; and Bank of Jamaica for
Jamaica's 2001 figure on FDI inflows.

The repatriation of profits represents the most prevalent factor causing FDI outflows to other countries. These flows fluctuated significantly during the last decade from US$37 million in 1990 to a peak of US$94.9 million in 1999.

## 1.2. Country of origin and destination

Firms from several countries have been very active in Jamaica. The mining sector was until recently concentrated among US and Canadian investors. However, with the arrival of Swiss-based Glencore in 2001, the number of players has increased. In telecom, the United Kingdom with Cable and Wireless, Ireland with Digicel, and the United States with Centennial Digital Corporation are the key players. The financial services sector comprises firms from Canada (such as Bank of Nova Scotia, CIBC, and National Commercial Bank), the United States (e.g. CITIBANK), and Trinidad and Tobago (Union Bank). The United States tops the list of the foreign investors with companies in sectors such as accounting, advertising, agribusiness and beverages, banking and finance, chemicals and pharmaceuticals, computer and data processing, consumer products, courier services, insurance, manufacturing and assembly, mining and energy, and tourism and hospitality industry. New players also include Spain in the tourism sector with, for example, Rui International Hotels in Negril. Dragados, a Spanish-based construction and services firm, is also helping managing the Montego Bay airport. The French have also been quite active recently. Bouygues, the French construction group selected to build the government's flagship project – Highway 2000 – has undertaken to finance 72 per cent of the US$390-million project. The road developer is expected to earn returns on its investment by charging tolls for use of the highway under a 35-year agreement. Bouygues has contracted ASF from France to assist in building and operating the proposed toll road system. Sogea, another French firm that constructed a water treatment plant in Negril for the National Water Commission, is also returning to the island in the Great River/Lucea Water Supply project, while Gregori International, also out of France, built the golf course for the Ritz Carlton Hotel in Montego Bay. Another French firm, Total, is currently prospecting for business opportunities in the local petroleum industry.

Jamaica has also become an outward investor. In fact, outward investment almost doubled between 1994 and 1999, from J$ 53 million to J$ 95 million. Some Jamaican companies such as Grace Kennedy and Co. have long been established abroad.[2]

## 1.3. Distribution by economic activity

In addition to the telecom and IT sector which has become one of the fastest growing sectors in Jamaica, other segments of the economy receiving FDI include mining, tourism, and textiles. Financial services, as shown in the next section, also represents a key sector for FDI, whereas agribusiness is growing.

### Telecommunications

Jamaica has a 100 per cent digital telecommunications network. The country's advanced telecommunications infrastructure is one of the most resilient and highest capacity telecom backbones in the region. Having identified telecommunications and technology as critical to Jamaica's development, the Government started a three-phased liberalization of the telecommunications industry in 1999. The new Telecommunications Act is based on pro-competitive principles. As a first step to liberalize the telecom sector, the Government of Jamaica issued two licenses for nearly US$100 million to foreign companies to operate mobile telephone networks. US-based Centennial Digital Jamaica and Irish-owned Digicel, which respectively paid US$45 million and US$47.5 million, hold these licenses.

### IT sector

Jamaica's Information Technology (IT) sector has experienced radical growth over the past five years spurred by substantial investment in the country's telecommunications infrastructure and the delivery of IT services. Information technology is now perceived as being one of Jamaica's most lucrative industries and the sector employs well over 6 000 persons.

OECD INVESTMENT POLICY REVIEWS – ISBN 92-64-10509-3 – © OECD 2004

Jamaica is a premier near shore investment location and has earned an international reputation for service and efficiency. The island provides a diverse number of informatics services, which ranges from basic data entry to multimedia and software development services.

Most of the companies in the IT sector are located either in the Montego Bay Free Zone area or the Kingston Metropolitan area. Both areas are in close proximity to shipping, airport facilities and support services. The Montego Bay Free Zone is particularly conducive to investments in the information technology sector due to the presence of Jamaica Digiport International (JDI), which holds powerful data transfer facilities for international exchanges as well as sophisticated imaging, voice and facsimile services. Jamaica Digiport International Ltd. is a fully owned subsidiary of Cable and Wireless Jamaica, which has significantly enhanced the country's ability to offer an impressive range of telecommunication services. With facilities that offer high-speed voice and data transmission through fibre, Jamaica Digiport guarantees the delivery of state of the art telecom services to an international clientele.

## Mining

In mining, nearly one-third of Jamaica's refining capacity changed ownership when Glencore, the Switzerland-based commodities trading group, bought Canadian-owned Alcan's two Jamaican alumina refineries in 2001. Jamaica has excellent prospects in the non-metallic mineral sector, which offer several lucrative opportunities in trade and investments. Jamaica is noted for its bauxite both in its crude form and that converted from alumina. However, a large and significant concentration of high purity limestone reserves, marble, riverstone, gypsum and anhydrite deposits are complimented by numerous mineral springs across the island. Suitable clays are also readily available in Jamaica to produce commercial quantities of fine ceramics and building components. Economic quantities of gold are also present in central Jamaica in the parish of Clarendon. Mining began in early 2000 and since March 2001, over 1 000 ounces of this precious metal has been exported. There are some major advantages to be gained from activities in this sector: the accessibility of mineral resources through surface mining; the strategic location to the large export markets of the world; trade being facilitated through multilateral and bilateral agreements.

The chemical sector in Jamaica is mainly distributive in nature, with a few manufacturers of bulk industrial chemicals, *e.g.* sulphuric acid, acetylene, sodium chloride, etc. The tropical marine climate of Jamaica coupled with strong ocean currents and consistent wind pattern in various areas of Jamaica, make the exploitation of alternate sources of energy a realistic goal and prime investment opportunity. Areas being exploited include wind, solar, hydro-power and biomass, among others.

## Tourism

In recent years, Jamaica has been ranked within the top five of the world's most favored tourist destinations. The significant contribution that the tourism sector has made to the economy is reflected in the strong Government support through the establishment of a number of technical support teams. In addition to a Ministry of Tourism there exists two other offices given the mandate of developing a growth path for tourism in Jamaica.

First, the Tourism Office within the Office of the Prime Minister is an overseer to all the organisations within the industry established to develop the tourism product, such as the Jamaica Tourist Board (JTB) and the Tourism Product Development Company (TDPCo). Secondly, JAMPRO, Jamaica's export and investment promotion agency, also has a Leisure Industry Department responsible for the promotion, development and facilitation of investments within the sector.

## Apparel

The apparel sector grew phenomenally growth during the period 1983 to 1996 to the point where it recorded the largest increase in non-traditional exports. The value of exports generated by the sector amounted to US$7.1 million in 1980 and peaked at US$535.68 million in 1996. There were some 80 manufacturing entities of which thirty-six were exporters, employing approximately 7 000 workers in 2001.

The Government is currently pursuing policies to transform the sector from basic assembly type to full packaged production-going up-market. This will require more value-added processes, fabric supplies and more efficient workers, if local apparel firms are to be able to form partnerships with US-based firms. These firms are requiring full packaged partners, expeditious style changes through the utilization of modern technology and quick turn around time at minimum cost. One of the single most important elements in ensuring access to the US market and the development of the local industry is the type of rules of origin existing in the textiles and apparel sectors. The soon-to-be-concluded Free Trade Area of the Americas represents an opportunity in that regard. More liberal rules of origin which would allow for non-US (but made in FTAA) inputs would greatly benefit the Caribbean Basin, including Jamaican, industry.

The Government has therefore embarked on Modernization of Industry Program to help the sector to become more technology driven and efficient. The replacement of obsolete machinery and equipment is an integral part of this program. The European Union-funded Trade Development Project has also been helping Jamaican firms to improve their competitiveness. Although these initiatives have contributed to a revitalization of the sector, the Government plans to implement a productivity incentive and cost reduction scheme, to give companies incentives linked to productivity.

Clustering around the transhipment ports in Kingston, Montego Bay, as well as at the air cargo airport, which will be built at Vernamfield, will also be pursued to encourage investments into the sector.

Table 1.3. **Foreign direct investment by sector, 1990-2000**
Millions of US dollars

|      | Manufacturing | | Agriculture | | Services | |
| --- | --- | --- | --- | --- | --- | --- |
|      | Absolute | Relative (%) | Absolute | Relative (%) | Absolute | Relative (%) |
| 1997 | 5.57  | 10.56 | 0.23 | 0.44 | 34.43  | 65.25 |
| 1998 | 5.62  | 7.44  | 6.79 | 9.00 | 50.99  | 67.50 |
| 1999 | 11.50 | 14.00 | 0.94 | 1.14 | 38.42  | 46.76 |
| 2000 | 37.40 | 20.23 | 0.30 | 0.16 | 113.13 | 61.20 |

Source: OECD.

## 1.4. Main foreign investors

There are nine foreign-owned firms among the fifteen largest Jamaican-based companies, as measured by the turnover in year 2000. Air Jamaica was unequivocally the largest Jamaican company during that year, whereas UK-based Cable and Wireless, which lost its monopoly on international communications on March 1, 2003, had the largest income among foreign investors. Moreover, a number of companies have changed ownership since the year 2000. Jamaica Public Service Co. (JPSCo) was privatized and sold to Atlanta-based Mirant Corp. in March 2001. Several financial institutions, which experienced serious problems, were revamped and sold to foreign investors. National Commercial Bank was bought by Canadian-based AIC in March 2002, whereas Union Bank was sold to Trinidad-based RTTB in 2001.

## 1.5. Main explanatory factors for FDI

Several factors have contributed to the increase in foreign direct investment in Jamaica over the past decade. The restructuring of a number of financial institutions starting in 1997, the liberalization of the telecom sector since 1999, the privatization of Government-owned public companies, the phenomenal growth in the tourism industry, as well as a myriad of incentives have a played a key role in attracting foreign investment to Jamaica.

### Market-seeking FDI in Jamaica

Jamaica has recently benefited from a large influx of market-seeking FDI in numerous services sectors with the liberalization of the telecom sector and

Table 1.4. **Jamaica's fifteen largest companies, based on turnover[1]**

| Company | Investor/country of origin | Sector(s) |
|---|---|---|
| 1. Air Jamaica | Jamaica | Provider of air transport |
| 2. Cable and Wireless Jamaica | Cable and Wireless, United Kingdom | Provider of domestic and international telecommunication services |
| 3. Jamaica Public Service Co. (JPSCo) | Owned by US-based Mirant Corp. since March 2001 | Supplier of electricity and power |
| 4. Bank of Nova Scotia | Bank of Nova Scotia, Canada | Commercial, merchant banking, and trust company operations |
| 5. Grace Kennedy and Co. | Jamaica | Merchandising of food, hardware and lumber, building and construction supplies, cosmetics, pharmaceuticals, and other items |
| 6. National Commercial Bank | Owned since March 2002 by Canadian-based AIC, a fund management company | Commercial banking operations |
| 7. Alumina Partners of Jamaica (Alpart) | US-based Kaiser Aluminium | Manufacturer and exporter of alumina |
| 8. Jamaica Producers Group | Jamaica | Marketing and distribution of bananas and other fresh produce; agricultural production, shipping and investment holdings |
| 9. Alcan Jamaica Co. | Sold by Canadian-based ALCAN to Swiss-based Glencore in June 2001 | Manufacturer and exporter of alumina |
| 10. Lascelles De Mercado | Jamaica | Cultivators of sugar cane and manufacturer of sugar and rum |
| 11. Alcoa Minerals, which jointly owned an alumina refinery (JAMALCO) with the Government of Jamaica | US-based Alcoa | Manufacturer and exporter of alumina |
| 12. Life of Jamaica | Jamaica | Life insurance |
| 13. Union Bank | Trinidad-based RBTT | Financial services (banking) |
| 14. Desnoes and Geddes (Red Stripe) | Irish-based Guinness Brewery | Beer |
| 15. Jamaica Broilers Group | Jamaica | Producers and suppliers of meat protein and animal feeds |

1. The information on the turnover was extracted from Business Observer, July 8, 2001.
*Source:* OECD.

the arrival of foreign-owned companies to operate mobile telephone networks. Internet service providers and call centres have also been recently established by foreign companies. Moreover, as mentioned above, the restructuring of the financial services system has led to the acquisition in March 2002 of the largest Jamaican commercial bank by a Canadian fund management company, and of another important financial institution, Union Bank, by Trinidad and Tobago's largest bank, RTTB one year earlier in March 2001. The privatization of numerous Jamaican Government entities

OECD INVESTMENT POLICY REVIEWS – ISBN 92-64-10509-3 – © OECD 2004

such as JPSCo, the electricity and power company, attracted foreign capital. Finally, tourism, which was traditionally Jamaican-owned, has become a key sector for foreign investors, including newcomers such as Spain.

### Natural-resource seeking FDI in Jamaica

The percentage of FDI geared towards extracting natural resources is significant in Jamaica. The mining sector is the second most important generator of foreign exchange, after tourism. Bauxite and alumina production represent more than 50 per cent of Jamaica's merchandise exports. Multinationals such as Kaiser, Alcoa, and Alcan (whose two refineries are now owned by Glencore) have long been established in the country. Other mining products of importance include non-metallic materials, such as limestone/lime, marble and gypsum.

### Efficiency-seeking FDI in Jamaica

Efficiency-seeking investment in Jamaica is concentrated in three free zones. The Montego Bay Free Zone has more than 450 000 sq. ft of factory, office and information processing space. It specializes in data entry, telemarketing and electronic firms. The Kingston Free Zone is located near the Kingston Harbor. Apparel, pharmaceutical, electronic, and ethanol businesses are established in that zone. The Garmex zone, located in the industrial section of Kingston, includes apparel and footwear companies. It is worth emphasizing that unable to compete with low-cost producers in Central America and Mexico and burdened by an overvalued exchange rate, the once flourishing apparel sector has suffered a severe contraction since the mid-1990s.

Several information technology companies, including call centres, are located in the Portmore Informatics Park. There is also a number of stand-alone free zones in the country.

## 1.6. Economic impact and linkages with the local economy

There is no data on the number of jobs that are directly the result of foreign direct investment in Jamaica. It is clear, however, that this number has been increasing steadily during the last decade with the boom in the tourism industry, the restructuring of the financial services sector, the recent liberalization of the telecom sector, and the privatization of numerous state-owned enterprises.

FDI linkages with the local Jamaican economy have been particularly strong in the tourism industry. Local restaurants and clubs, as well as the retail and distributive services sectors have also benefited from the fast growth in the tourism industry. The creation of an informatics park has helped the country reap the benefits of the information technology revolution.

The FDI-GDP ratio has grown rapidly since the mid-1990s, from 2.86 per cent in 1995 to 6.61 per cent in 2000.

## 1.7. Future perspectives

The People's National Party (PNP) gained an unprecedented fourth consecutive term of office in the last general election held on October 16, 2002. Prime Minister P.J. Patterson saw his majority reduced to eight seats in the 60-seat parliament. His previous administration had a 38-seat majority. No significant policy changes are envisaged with respect to foreign direct investment but policymaking may prove to be more challenging on issues such as restoring the fiscal balance and reducing poverty, crime, and unemployment.

OECD INVESTMENT POLICY REVIEWS – ISBN 92-64-10509-3 – © OECD 2004

ISBN 92-64-10509-3
OECD Investment Policy Reviews
Caribbean Rim: Costa Rica, Dominican Republic and Jamaica
© OECD 2004

# Chapter 2

# Investment Environment

## 2.1. Structure of the economy

Jamaica's real gross domestic product experienced positive growth for a third consecutive year in 2002. After posting a rate of 0.7 per cent in 2000, GDP grew by 1.7 per cent in 2001 and 0.6 per cent in 2002. Several factors contributed to the slow growth of the economy in 2001-2002. The fiscal deficit limited the Government's ability to spur demand. Flood damages in May 2002 and Hurricane Michelle in November 2001 adversely affected numerous crops, whereas the September 11, 2001 terrorist attacks on the United States impacted negatively on tourism, the country's main foreign exchange earner (approximately US$1.4 billion in 2000). Moreover, Jamaica was also beset by the closure in October 2001 – for three months – of JAMALCO Refinery – a joint venture between the Jamaican Government and Alcoa, following a strike at this alumina processing plant.[3]

The services sector accounts for a total of more than 70 per cent of Jamaica's GDP (in current prices) and is undoubtedly the most dynamic sector of the Jamaican economy. Although tourism experienced a decline in 2001, numerous projects aimed at promoting the diversification of the tourism industry have been put in place by the Government and JAMPRO – the Jamaican Government agency responsible for promoting and processing investment proposals – in order to take advantage of the country's full potential in that sector. Hotels, restaurants, and clubs have benefited significantly from this increase in tourism, as shown in Table 2.1.

Retail and distributive trade continues to be a sector in expansion, whereas the transport, storage and communication sector has grown at a fast pace since the mid-1990s. The real GDP for transport storage and the telecommunication sector increased by an impressive 6.3 per cent in 2001. The expansion of the Jamaica Urban Transit Company and the increase in cargo and ship activities at the port contributed to this high growth rate. The implementation of the second phase in the liberalization of the telecom sector in 2001 with the granting of new licences also played a significant role in boosting the growth rate of this sector. Irish-owned Digicel and Centennial Digital Jamaica – a subsidiary of US giant Centennial Communications – began offering mobile service in 2001. The monopoly of the UK-based Cable and Wireless in the phone market, which ended in March 2003, will lead to further growth in the sector.

OECD INVESTMENT POLICY REVIEWS – ISBN 92-64-10509-3 – © OECD 2004

Table 2.1. **Gross Domestic Product by sector in producers' values
at constant 1986 prices**

In percentage of GDP in producers' values

| | 1996 | 1997 | 1998 | 1999 | 2000 (est.) |
|---|---|---|---|---|---|
| **Origin of GDP** | | | | | |
| Agriculture, forestry, and fishing | 9.2 | 8.0 | 8.0 | 8.1 | 7.1 |
| Mining and quarrying | 8.6 | 9.1 | 9.4 | 9.3 | 9.1 |
| Bauxite/alumina | 8.5 | 8.9 | 9.3 | 9.2 | 9.0 |
| Manufacturing | 16.7 | 16.6 | 15.9 | 15.9 | 15.8 |
| Food (excluding sugar) | 3.2 | 3.2 | 3.2 | 3.3 | 3.4 |
| Petroleum refining | 1.7 | 1.9 | 1.8 | 1.8 | 1.8 |
| Alcoholic beverages | 1.6 | 1.6 | 1.6 | 1.5 | 1.6 |
| Textiles and apparel | 1.1 | 0.9 | 0.8 | 0.6 | 0.6 |
| Sugar, molasses, and rum | 0.5 | 0.5 | 0.4 | 0.5 | 0.4 |
| Construction | 8.4 | 8.2 | 7.7 | 7.7 | 7.6 |
| Services | | | | | |
| Distributive trade | 19.7 | 20.3 | 20.1 | 20.0 | 20.0 |
| Transport, storage and communication | 12.7 | 13.7 | 14.5 | 15.8 | 16.9 |
| Financing and insurance services | 14.0 | 11.7 | 11.5 | 13.6 | 14.9 |
| Hotels, restaurants, and clubs | 7.9 | 8.3 | 8.6 | 8.8 | 9.2 |
| Real estate and business services | 9.2 | 9.0 | 8.9 | 8.9 | 8.8 |
| Government services | 6.2 | 6.4 | 6.5 | 6.5 | 6.4 |
| Electricity and water | 4.4 | 4.8 | 5.1 | 5.4 | 5.5 |

Source: International Monetary Fund, *Jamaica: Statistical Appendix*, June 2001.

The contribution of the financing and insurance services sector to the GDP is growing again after the Government decided to intervene and the sector underwent major restructuring, beginning in 1997. The Government created FINSAC (Financial Sector Adjustment Company), with the objective of restoring liquidity and solvency to the banking and insurance sectors, protecting policyholders and pensioners, and strengthening these sectors through stronger regulation. FINSAC swapped bad debt, and took over and closed a number of banks and financial institutions. For example, in 1999, it merged four commercial banks, five merchant banks and four building societies to establish Union Bank, which was sold in 2001 to RTTB, Trinidad and Tobago's largest bank. The National Commercial Bank (NCB), Jamaica's largest commercial bank, was restructured in 2000 and sold in early 2002 to AIC, a Canadian company. In October 2002, the World Bank approved three loans for Jamaica totalling US$129.8 million. The first loan of US$75 million helped convert all remaining liabilities at FINSAC into tradable loans, therefore closing FINSAC operations.

Agriculture accounted for 7.3 per cent of total real GDP in 2001, having increased by 5.2 per cent (1986 prices) mainly as a result of an increase in hectares of crop production. But the sector was severely affected in the last quarter of 2001 by flood rains that took place in November. Extensive flooding also occurred in May and June of 2002, leading to significant losses for farmers. The country had also seen a substantial decline in agricultural output in the late 1990s, following a severe drought caused by El Niño. As a whole, the contribution of the agriculture, forestry and fishing sector to the GDP, as measured in producers' values at constant 1986 prices, declined from 9.2 per cent in 1996 to 7.1 per cent in 2000. The value of agricultural exports grew by 7.9 per cent in 2001 to reach US$151.9 million. Traditional exports recorded a decline of 11 per cent, whereas non-traditional exports grew by 23.6 per cent. Sugar cane remains the single most important Jamaican crop. The industry has often been unable during the last few years to meet its sugar quota set by the Lomé Convention (now the Cotonou Agreement). The Government has had to import sugar and financially support private producers. The sugar industry employs approximately 28 000 people plus 13 000 seasonal workers. In addition to coffee production and the internationally popular Blue Mountain coffee blend, roots and tubers, as well as fruits are the other main agricultural crops.

The mining and quarrying sector captured 9.1 per cent of total real GDP in 2001 and enjoyed a growth rate of 3.8 per cent (real GDP). As in the case of agriculture, this increase reversed the decline in real terms that the sector had experienced during the previous two years. A strike at JAMALCO Refinery led to the closure of the plant for three months and a decline in the exports of alumina. As exports of crude bauxite grew during 2001, total mining exports remained virtually stable compared to the year 2000. Jamaica is the third largest producer of bauxite ore in the world after Australia and Guinea. The bauxite and alumina industries employ more than 4 000 people. The quarrying industry, which includes gypsum, marble, silica and clays, enjoyed an increase in its output in 2001, in large part due to the growth in road construction and repairs.

The manufacturing sector grew at the modest rate of 0.6 per cent in 2001 to represent 15.5 per cent of total real GDP. Food processing and beverages were the major driving force of the manufacturing sector, whereas chemicals and textiles and apparel continued to suffer closure of plants and factories. The textiles and apparel sector has faced major competition from Mexican producers since the implementation of the North American Free Trade Agreement (NAFTA) in 1994 and from Central American low-cost producer countries in the context of the Caribbean Basin Initiative (CBI). As shown in Table 2.1, its share of the Jamaican GDP has been declining for several years. An overvalued exchange rate has also eroded Jamaica's competitiveness in this sector. Other manufacturing industries include sugar, molasses, and rum; machineries and tools; metal products; glass; and cement. Manufacturing exports declined in 2001.

The construction sector benefited from the modernization of the road infrastructure and the reconstruction which followed the damage caused by floods at the end of 2001. The sector, whose share of real GDP has remained practically unchanged since 1998, recorded a growth rate of 2 per cent in 2001.

On the macroeconomic front, the country has been growing in real terms since the beginning of 2000, after having contracted in the mid-1990s. The total public debt, which will remain a challenge for the years to come, increased in the late 1990s with the bailouts of numerous financial services institutions. The total debt represented 79.1 per cent of GDP in Fiscal Year 1996/97[4] and 145 per cent of GDP at the beginning of 2003. This increase has been shouldered by domestic financing (85 per cent) and also by the external debt, which accounted for approximately 60 per cent of GDP in early 2003.

The prospects for growth are good for the Jamaican economy, albeit they are, in part, dependent on the recovery of the US economy, Jamaica's main trading partner. The liberalization of the telecom sector, the restructuring of the financial services sector and the privatization of numerous infrastructure public services are vital components for the efficient operation of the economy. They will contribute to increasing the competitiveness of other sectors such as tourism and manufacturing, and allow Jamaica to play a greater role as a small but active player on the international scene.

As mentioned above, three shocks (civil disturbances in Kingston in July 2001, the terrorist attacks on the United States on September 11, and the flood rains in November 2001 which damaged one fifth of Jamaica's crop acreage) had a considerable impact on Jamaica's fiscal revenue in 2001. For the first nine months of Fiscal Year (FY) 2001/02 (i.e. from April to December 2001), expenditures increased by J$ 17.9 billion over the corresponding period during the previous year, whereas revenue grew only by J$ 1.9 billion. Much of the increase in revenue came from the sale of the Jamaica Public Services Company Limited (JPSCo.), Jamaica's primary source of electricity.

The Government, which is targeting a deficit of 4.4 per cent of GDP, excluding income from divestments, in Fiscal Year 2002/03, may have a hard time meeting its objective. In 2002, revenue from the tourism industry, which generates a large amount of direct and indirect tax revenue, fell below expectations, whereas increase in local tax for electricity bills and property valuation were postponed or reversed. In fact, for the first six months of FY 2002/03, tax revenue fell 13 per cent short of the Government's original projection.

The public sector fiscal deficit, which represented as much as 11.1 per cent of GDP in FY 1998/99, remains a challenge for the Jamaican administration. Divestment proceeds from the sale of public sector enterprises have helped finance the public sector fiscal few years but as there are fewer entities to privatize the Government will have to devise new ways to boost revenues and keep expenditures in check.

The current account deficit, which increased to reach 10.1 per cent of GDP in 2001 continued to deteriorate in 2002 due to external shocks and a sharp fall in tourist expenditure after September 11, 2001. A rise in interest payments has also led to the worsening of the current account deficit. Tourism recovery and increase in export earnings should contribute to lower this ratio in 2003.

Table 2.2. **Central government revenues and expenditures**

As a percentage of GDP

|  | 1996/97 | 1997/98 | 1998/99 | 1999/00 | 2000/01 (est.) |
|---|---|---|---|---|---|
| **Total revenues** | **26.4** | **25.8** | **27.1** | **30.5** | **30.8** |
| **Total expenditures** | **31.9** | **33.5** | **34.1** | **34.8** | **31.8** |
| *of which:* | | | | | |
| Interest | 11.4 | 9.5 | 12.7 | 14.1 | 13.1 |
| Savings | 0.1 | −2.7 | −4.3 | −1.2 | 1.9 |
| Public sector primary balance | 6.8 | 1.3 | 7.1 | 11.0 | 12.6 |
| Public sector balance | −4.6 | −9.4 | −11.1 | −7.4 | −5.3 |
| Domestic financing | 5.5 | 8.3 | 11.9 | 8.5 | 1.6 |
| Banking system | −1.2 | 18.9 | 8.6 | 2.9 | 4.3 |
| Others (incl. divestment proceeds) | 6.7 | −10.6 | 3.3 | 5.6 | −2.7 |
| Foreign financing | −0.9 | 1.1 | −0.8 | −1.2 | 3.7 |

Source: International Monetary Fund, *Jamaica: Statistical Appendix*, June 2001.

Table 2.3. **Current account balance**

In percentage of GDP

|  | 1996/97 | 1997/98 | 1998/99 | 1999/00 |
|---|---|---|---|---|
| Current account balance | −1.4 | −5.4 | −3.0 | −4.3 |
| Goods balance | −14.9 | −15.9 | −15.0 | −16.2 |
| Exports | 24.6 | 23.6 | 20.9 | 21.0 |
| Imports | 39.5 | 39.5 | 36.0 | 37.2 |
| Services | 7.3 | 6.5 | 7.3 | 7.5 |
| Income | −3.4 | −4.4 | −3.8 | −5.0 |
| Transfers | 9.6 | 8.5 | 8.6 | 9.4 |

Source: International Monetary Fund, *Jamaica: Statistical Appendix*, June 2001.

## 2.2. Infrastructure

The following section covers some of the most important infrastructure networks in Jamaica: the road and rail network, naval transport, air transport, telecommunications, and energy.

### Road and rail network

Jamaica's national road web is comprised of approximately 5 000 kilometers of main roads and 11 000 kilometers of parochial roads. Approximately 12 000 kilometers are paved. The highway system is in need of improvement, and various projects for the renewal and maintenance of roads have been put into work. In total, the Government's FY01/02 budget allocated to roadwork was of J$ 2 billion.

One of the main road projects initiated in 1999 was the construction of the first phase of North Coast highway, linking the principal coastal tourist sites of Montego Bay and Negril. After land acquisition problems and the withdrawal of the first Korean contractor Bosung Engineering and Construction Co. Ltd., the Jamaican Government awarded a contract for the second phase (97 kilometers between Montego Bay and Ocho Rios) to Argentine contractor José Cartellone Construcciones Civiles.

As mentioned earlier, in July 2001, the French firm Bouygues Travaux was awarded a $390 million contract to build the first phase of "Highway 2000", a six lane bridge from Kingston to Portmore plus 74 kilometers of four-lane highway. Eventually, "Highway 2000" will link the cities of Kingston and Montego Bay, becoming a principal road across the island. In November 2002, the French company ASF, which develops and operates toll roads in the south of France, announced that it was taking a one-third stake in TransJamaica Highway, the vehicle being used by Bouygues, to develop and manage Jamaica's first toll road in the south-central part of Jamaica.

The rail network coverage of Jamaica is 272 kilometers. The Government has signed an agreement with Rail India Technical and Economic Services Ltd. (RITES) to rehabilitate and upgrade the island's rail system.

### Naval transport infrastructure

Jamaica has two world-class international seaports–Port of Kingston and Port of Montego Bay–and a number of smaller, specialized ports and harbors including Alligator Pond, Discovery Bay, Ocho Rios, Port Antonio, Rocky Point, and Port Esquivel. Kingston Harbour is the seventh natural harbor in the world with 21 square kilometers of navigable water. Ports are both privately and publicly administered. Kingston transhipment port, which handles approximately 80 per cent of all imports to the island, underwent expansion to increase docking capacity in 2001, at a cost of $120 million. Facilities have also been recently upgraded in Ocho Rios, Montego Bay, and Port Antonio.

Jamaica is located in the centre of the main shipping lanes through the Panama Canal. This makes the island very attractive to international shipping companies and as such, there are over 30 international shipping lines operating in the island and linking Jamaica with the rest of the world. The main shipping lines include Zim, Evergreen, Maersk, Jamaica Producers, Happag Lloyd, Ned Lloyd and Kent Lines.

Customs clearance procedures last approximately 48 hours. On average, it will take three days for a shipment to reach the premises of the company of the importer after the ship has docked in the port.

### Air transport infrastructure

Jamaica has a total of thirty-five airports. Two of these are major international airports, Norman Manley International Airport located in Kingston and Sangster International Airport (SIA) located in Montego Bay. The Norman Manley Airport is mainly used by Jamaica's local residents and business travellers, and has a capacity of approximately 500 passengers per hour. The Sangster Airport caters mainly to tourists and has a capacity of 1 242 passengers per hour. Domestic air travel is facilitated namely through the aerodromes of Tinson Pen (Kingston), Ken Jones (Portland), Boscobel (St. Mary), and Negril (Westmoreland).

All airports in Jamaica are publicly administered, with the exception of Norman Manley International Airport, and recently privatized (January 2003) Sangster International Airport in Montego Bay. The Jamaican Government will continue to own the Sangster airport property and will have the right to terminate the concession to Vancouver Airport Services of Canada in the event that the private operator fails to meet his contractual obligations. Eleven major international airlines operate in Jamaica, including American Airlines, Air Canada, British Airways, Trinidad-based BWIA, USAirways, Panama-based COPA, ALM Antillean Airline, and Northwest Airlines. The main provider of domestic travel is Air Jamaica Express. Both international airports offer cargo facilities and air cargo services.

### Infrastructure in telecommunications and energy

Basic telecommunication services in Jamaica are provided by the Government of Jamaica with Cable and Wireless of Jamaica Limited – C&WJ, whose main shareholder – Cable and Wireless (UK) – control 82 per cent of C&WJ. Under an agreement signed in 1999 to begin a phased end to C&W's stranglehold on Jamaica's telecommunications sector, the company was allowed to maintain a three-year exclusive position as a carrier of international voice, the most lucrative part of its business. As mentioned previously, C&WJ lost its monopoly on international communications on March 1, 2003.

Jamaica's telecommunication sector is booming, with the expenditure of J$ 30 billion by the island's three mobile telephone companies over the period 2000-2002 and the expansion in the number of cellular and fixed phone lines to 1.4 million. There are 900 000 cellular phone lines and 500 000 fixed lines in Jamaica. Installation of phone lines have in the past taken place seven working days after the receipt of an application in the case of business customers, and fourteen days after the receipt of an application in the case of residential customers. Approximately 4.5 faults are estimated to occur per 100 phone lines per year.

The call centres (or telemarketing) component of the information technology (IT) industry has also been progressing. Three new call centres were established in the Spring of 2002. These include the New Kingston-based Jamswitch with 48 employees; the Montego Bay-based Teleservices Direct, employing 72 people, and Inter-Sat, which is also based in Montego Bay and has 34 employees. Two other companies – Sitel Caribbean and Affiliated Computer Services – are expanding their operations. The Government of Jamaica also recently announced that a US$20 million loan from the Inter-American Development Bank would be used to implement an Internet-based communication system to enable the electronic payment of a range of taxes, customs duties and other Government charges.

The interest of the Canadian-based telecommunications firm, the Goldline Group, in Jamaica's Internet and domestic voice telecommunication service is worth noting. The Goldline Group is Canada's largest provider of prepaid long distance calling cards servicing almost 80 per cent of that market. Established in 1991, the Goldline Group will join another Canadian firm, Hemitel, in Jamaica's telecommunications industry. Hemitel Incorporated has been competing with Cable and Wireless Jamaica (C&WJ) for voice service since October 2001 when it launched its Irie Vibes international calling card. It expanded into local services earlier this year. Hemitel and Goldline are just two of the 69 recipients of local and international voice carrier licenses issued by the Ministry of Commerce and Technology, as of March 2002, for operation in the local telecommunications industry. Hemitel, which has registered offices in Jamaica, was granted its international and local voice service provider licenses in April and November 2001 respectively.

Also worth noting is that the Government of Jamaica planned to establish a one-stop regulatory agency to govern the converging information and telecommunication sectors in light of the full liberalization of the industry in 2003. One of the issues to be addressed in the new policy framework is the role of several regulatory agencies such as the Spectrum Management Authority, the Broadcasting Commission, the Office of Utilities Regulation (OUR) and the University of the West Indies (UWI) which administers the .jm domain, in light of the convergence of telecommunication, broadcasting and Internet technologies.

Table 2.4. **Telecommunications country profile: Jamaica**

| | |
|---|---|
| Telephone density | 19.73 per 100 inhabitants (2001) |
| Cellular density | 26.94 per 100 inhabitants (2001) |
| Equipment market size | $64.3 million (2000) |
| US telecom equipment exports | $72.24 million (2001) |
| Telecom services revenue | $462.6 million (2000) |
| WTO basic telecom services agreement signatory | Yes |

*Source:* Telecommunications Country Profile, US Department of Commerce.

### Electricity and power

Over 95 per cent of electrical power in Jamaica is generated from imported fuel oil. The principal producer and distributor of electricity in the island, Jamaica Public Service Company (JPSCo.), was privatized and sold to Atlanta-based Mirant Corp. in March 2001. In 1999, the annual production of electricity in the island was 6.53 billion kwh, of which 92.28 per cent was produced from fossil fuel; 1.36 per cent from hydro energy; and 6.36 per cent from other sources (but none from nuclear energy). The electricity consumption for that year amounted to 6.073 billion kwh.

## 2.3. Human capital

The labor force in Jamaica consisted of approximately 1 100 000 persons in 2001. The labor force participation rate declined as it has during the last few years. The unemployment rate, which is generally higher among women, was of 15 per cent, more specifically 10.3 per cent for males and 21 per cent for females. The services sector's share of employment grew to reach 63 per cent of total employment, whereas the goods-producing sector saw its share decline by 1.6 per cent.

Under the laws of Jamaica, an employer must observe the regulation regarding the statutory national minimum wage, which increased by 50 per cent in January 2002 to reach J$ 1 800 per 40-hour week. The minimum wage varies according to sectors. For example, industrial guard services now receive J$ 2 828 per 40-hour week, an increase of 40 per cent compared to 2001.

Firing practices are also subject to industrial and labor laws. An employer may terminate an employment contract for a specific reason provided that he gives the worker advanced notice, or, alternatively, pay in lieu of notice.

Statutory notice spans from two weeks for employment under five years, to eight weeks for employment fifteen years and over. If the employment contract is terminated through redundancy, there is an additional statutory provision of three weeks severance pay for each year of service in excess of ten years.

Under the Jamaican Constitution, a Jamaican citizen enjoys "freedom of association". Therefore, there are no restrictions on trade unions or the right to strike except for certain rules that apply to essential services. The year 2001 was the best in the past ten years with respect to industrial relations, as reported by the *Planning Institute of Jamaica*. The number of work disruptions declined by 50 per cent to fourteen. The *Labour Relations and Industrial Disputes Act (LRIDA)* provides for conflict resolution mechanisms. If there are parties to a dispute who are unable to arrive at a settlement within a reasonable time, the dispute may be referred to the Industrial Dispute Tribunal for Resolution.

While education is provided by a number of public and private institutions, Jamaica needs to increase the number of its technical and tertiary-level education programs in order to train skilled workers capable to attract high value-added FDI. Moreover, better targeted training would also contribute to increase the productivity level of the Jamaican labor force. Although the average years of schooling of the non-professional workforce is estimated to be of eleven years, more remains to be done if the country intends to be a real player in the knowledge economy.[5]

Table 2.5. **Jamaica's labor force**

|  | 1997 | 1998 | 1999 | 2000 | 2001 |
|---|---|---|---|---|---|
| Labor force (000) | 1 133.8 | 1 128.6 | 1 119.1 | 1 105.3 | 1 104.8 |
| Male (000) | 613.8 | 614.3 | 611.7 | 615.0 | 618.1 |
| Female (000) | 520.0 | 514.2 | 507.4 | 490.3 | 486.7 |
| Labor force participation rate (%) | 66.5 | 65.6 | 64.5 | 63.3 | 63.0 |
| Male (%) | 74.6 | 73.9 | 73.0 | 73.0 | 73.0 |
| Female (%) | 59.0 | 57.8 | 56.6 | 54.3 | 53.6 |
| Total unemployment rate (%) | 16.5 | 15.5 | 15.7 | 15.5 | 15.0 |
| Male (%) | 10.6 | 10.0 | 10.0 | 10.2 | 10.3 |
| Female (%) | 23.5 | 22.1 | 22.5 | 22.3 | 21.0 |
| Average weekly earnings of all employees (1990 J$)[1] | 5 177.2 | 5 881.9 | 6 869.1 | 7 277.7 | n.a. |

1. From Survey of Employment, Earnings and Hours Worked in Large Establishments, Statistical Institute of Jamaica.

*Source:* Planning Institute of Jamaica (*www.pioj.gov.jm/statistics/statis_gdpi.stm*).

## 2.4. Public governance: transparency, integrity, and rule of law

For the past three years, Transparency International has not included Jamaica in its Corruption Perceptions Index. However, in 1999, when Jamaica was last included, it ranked 50th on the list of Transparency International, ahead of Mexico, Guatemala, Nicaragua, Argentina, Colombia, Venezuela, Bolivia, Ecuador and Honduras but behind Chile, Costa Rica, Peru, Uruguay, Brazil, and El Salvador (see Table 2.6). Many Jamaicans believe that corruption remains a major problem in the country and that it is rooted in the country's political culture. Jamaica is a signatory of the OECD convention on combating bribery and has ratified the Inter-American Convention Against Corruption. On March 11, 2003, the Government launched the Corruption Prevention Commission, which was established to detect, investigate and dispose of any acts of corruption among public servants. Under the Corruption Prevention Act of 2000, a public servant is defined as any person who is employed in the public, municipal or parochial service in Jamaica, in the service of a statutory body or authority or a government company. A public servant is appointed, elected, selected or otherwise engaged to perform a public function. The only public servants who must submit their annual statutory declarations are those who receive or earn emoluments in excess of the amount prescribed by the Minister of Justice. The amount that is now prescribed is J$ 2 million. members of Parliament, although required to submit annual statements, do so in accordance with the Parliament (Integrity of Members) Act.

Table 2.6. **1999 corruption perceptions index for Latin American and Caribbean countries**

| Country rank | | Score |
|---|---|---|
| 19 | Chile | 6.9 |
| 32 | Costa Rica | 5.1 |
| 40 | Peru | 4.5 |
| 41 | Uruguay | 4.4 |
| 45 | Brazil | 4.1 |
| 49 | El Salvador | 3.9 |
| **50** | **Jamaica** | **3.8** |
| 58 | Mexico | 3.4 |
| 68 | Guatemala | 3.2 |
| 70 | Nicaragua | 3.1 |
| 71 | Argentina | 3.0 |
| 72 | Colombia | 2.9 |
| 75 | Venezuela | 2.6 |
| 80 | Bolivia | 2.5 |
| 82 | Ecuador | 2.4 |
| 94 | Honduras | 1.8 |

*Source:* Transparency International (*www.transparency.org*).

OECD INVESTMENT POLICY REVIEWS – ISBN 92-64-10509-3 – © OECD 2004

The Government has undertaken a program of Reform of the Public Sector and the Public Service Staff Orders. The program includes modernization of a number of agencies. It aims to achieve improvements in efficiency and the quality of customer service.

The number of violent crimes continues to be a problem for Jamaica. In order to fight crime and improve the country's justice system, a total of J\$9.8 billion was devoted to Public Order and Safety Services in 2001. This new multifaceted approach aims at strengthening and reorganizing the Jamaican Constabulary Force (JCF), especially the Crime Management Unit, an elite crime-fighting unit within the JCF. The overall crime rate declined in 2001 from 1 507 per 100 000 inhabitants in year 2000 to 1 282 in 2001. The murder rate, however, increased from 34 to 43 per 100 000 inhabitants from year 2000 to 2001. Security cooperation between Jamaica, the United Kingdom and the United States has also led to specialized training to stem the flow of illegal weapons. Moreover, a number of new pieces of legislation seeking to improve the judicial process were tabled in Parliament.

A competition policy law was promulgated in Jamaica in 1993 and amended in 2001. The Fair Trading Commission (JFTC) was established as a specialized agency to administer the 1993 Fair Competition Act (FCA). The FCA provides for the maintenance and encouragement of competition in the conduct of trade, business and in the supply of services in Jamaica. The JFTC has the power to carry out investigations in relation to the conduct of business in Jamaica to determine if any enterprise is engaging in practices that are in contravention of the Act. Such investigations may be self-initiated by the JFTC or be carried out following a complaint. All investigations are carried out by the staff of the JFTC, which has the power to obtain any information that it considers necessary for the purposes of the investigation. Where necessary, an authorized officer of the JFTC may, with a warrant, enter and search any premises. The officer may remove any documents from the premises. Copies of documents removed may be made and the original must be returned within seven days. Also, the Commissioners have the power to summon and examine witnesses; to call for and examine documents; and to administer oaths. The JFTC can also take to Court any business or individual who has been found guilty of anti-competitive practice and has failed to take corrective measures, after being instructed by the Commissioners.[6]

The Jamaican judicial system is based on English common law and practice and consists of local courts, a Court appeal, and a Supreme Court. Final appeals are made to the Judicial Committee of the Privy Council in the United Kingdom. Discussions are currently taking place among a number of Caribbean nations, including Jamaica, with a view to establishing a Caribbean Court of Justice (CCJ) to replace the Judicial Committee of the Privy Council. In July 2002, CARICOM leaders mandated the Caribbean Development Bank

(CDB) to raise US$100 million for a trust fund to finance the proposed Caribbean Court of Justice. The CCJ is to have original jurisdiction in interpreting the CARICOM treaty, which officials say is critical for the functioning of a single market and economy – which the community intends to fully implement by 2005 – as well as to be the final court of appeal of several Caribbean countries.

## 2.5. Trade regime

Jamaica signed the General Agreement on Tariffs and Trade (GATT) on December 31, 1963 and has been a member of the World Trade Organization since its inception.[7] It has also been an active participant in the Free Trade Area of the Americas (FTAA) process since 1994. In addition, the country is participating in a number of other trade initiatives. Jamaica is an original member of the Caribbean Community and Common Market (CARICOM), established by the Treaty of Chaguaramas signed on July 4, 1973. CARICOM currently comprises 15 member states.[8] In 1989, the Heads of Government of the Caribbean Community agreed to deepen the integration process and determined that the Region would work towards the establishment of a single market and economy. The Caribbean Single Market and Economy (CSME) revolves around five main axes: the free movement of goods, services, and factors of production; the harmonization of laws and regulations affecting economic activities; the reform of CARICOM's institutions; the coordination of macroeconomic policies and foreign trade relations; and the implementation of a common external tariff with a maximum tariff of 20 per cent on non-agricultural goods and 40 per cent on agricultural goods. The Revised Treaty of Chaguaramas, which includes nine Protocols amending the original Treaty and which provides the legal framework for CARICOM to move to a Single Economy and Market, was signed by most CARICOM Heads of Government, including Jamaica's, when they met in July 2001 in The Bahamas.[9] On March 1, 2002, CARICOM member States agreed on a program with a timetable for the removal of existing restrictions impeding or infringing on the rights of CARICOM nationals to provide services, move capital and establish business enterprises. CARICOM members made the commitment to remove these restrictions progressively from 2003 to 2005.

Through its membership of CARICOM, Jamaica signed a trade agreement with Venezuela in October 1992 (which entered into force on January 1, 1993) and with Colombia in 1994 (which became effective on January 1, 1995), respectively. Both agreements were concluded under the provision for non-reciprocal partial scope agreements of the Latin American Integration Association (ALADI), of which Colombia and Venezuela are members. Certain CARICOM products are given duty-free access to Venezuela. Tariffs on a second group of goods are reduced in annual stages until reaching zero, and tariffs on

OECD INVESTMENT POLICY REVIEWS – ISBN 92-64-10509-3 – © OECD 2004

the remaining products receive most-favored-nation (MFN) treatment when they enter the Venezuelan market. The agreement with Colombia is very similar to that with Venezuela, except that it calls for "postponed reciprocity" where four CARICOM member States – Barbados, Guyana, Jamaica and Trinidad and Tobago, also known as the "more-developed countries" of CARICOM, must since June 1, 1998 grant duty-free access to some Colombian products.

CARICOM has also signed a free trade agreement with the Dominican Republic in 1998,[10] and a trade and economic agreement with Cuba in 2000, providing the framework for the promotion and expansion of trade between the member States of CARICOM and Cuba.[11] In March 2003, CARICOM and Costa Rica concluded a free trade agreement. Under this agreement, a wide range of products will be traded freely or at preferential rates although some sensitive products will be excluded from free trade. The duty on other products will be phased out over a four-year period beginning January 1, 2005. CARICOM countries, including Jamaica, have also expressed interest in negotiating a free trade agreement with Canada. On the occasion of the Canada-CARICOM Summit on January 19, 2001, in Montego Bay, Jamaica, Canada's Prime Minister Jean Chrétien and his CARICOM counterparts announced the launch of discussions towards the negotiation of a Canada-CARICOM free trade agreement.

Several industrialized countries have established a generalized system of preferences (GSP), which allows for duty concessions to exports originating in developing countries. The magnitude of the duty concession and the number of countries covered vary among countries. Jamaican products are accorded GSP benefits by Australia, Austria, Canada, the Czech Republic, the European Union, Japan, New Zealand, Poland, the Slovak Republic and Switzerland.

Jamaica also benefits from the unilateral preferential tariff treatment granted by the United States to countries qualifying under the 1983 Caribbean Basin Initiative (CBI), which was given new impetus with the Caribbean Basin Trade Partnership Act (CBTPA), effective since October 2000. The CBTPA will remain in effect until the earlier of two dates: September 30, 2008, or the date the Free Trade Area of the Americas enters into force.

Under the 1986 CARIBCAN agreement, Canada grants duty free access to goods (most products excluding textiles, clothing, footwear, luggage and other leather goods, lubricating oils, and methanol) from the Commonwealth Caribbean, including Jamaica, as long as they satisfy the specific requirements of rules of origin. That is, a minimum of 60 per cent of the price of the product must originate within the beneficiary country or in Canada.

Jamaica is also a member of the African, Caribbean and Pacific (ACP) group of states that benefit from the Cotonou agreement. The partnership agreement between these states and the European Union (EU) was signed in

Cotonou, Benin on June 23, 2000, as a successor agreement to the Lomé Trade and Aid Convention, which had provided the structure for trade and cooperation between the ACPs and the EU since 1975. On April 9, 2002, the European Commission adopted a negotiating strategy for Economic Partnership Agreements, the free trade areas that will replace preferential trading arrangements currently offered by the EU to its ACP partners. Negotiations will take place between September 27, 2002 and January 2008. The resulting agreement will enter into force in 2008, but will have a twelve-year transition period, i.e. until 2020. Until 2008 when the outcome of these negotiations is to be implemented, the current non-reciprocal tariff preferences will remain in place.

The preferential agreements signed by CARICOM members with United States, the European Union, and Canada have resulted in closer trade links between Jamaica and these countries, as shown in Tables 11 and 12. The United States is the single most important export market for Jamaica, accounting for 39.1 per cent of all Jamaican exports in 2000. It is important to point out here that this figure is undoubtedly underestimated by at least 15 per cent since it excludes free zone exports, which generally capture between 14 and 17 per cent of all exports. The European Union came second at 22.5 per cent and Canada third at 10.2 per cent. On the import side of the trade balance equation, US goods represented 44.8 per cent of Jamaican imports, whereas CARICOM accounted for 11.1 per cent, with Trinidad and Tobago representing 91 per cent of CARICOM's share. It is worth noting that Venezuela has become a key partner for Jamaica with respect to imports, particularly in crude oil, and that the EU import share has plummeted in recent years.

Table 2.7. **Exports to principal trading partners**
In percentage of total exports

|  | 1996 | 1997 | 1998 | 1999 | 2000 |
|---|---|---|---|---|---|
| Canada | 11.8 | 14.1 | 11.5 | 10.9 | 10.2 |
| CARICOM | 3.8 | 3.3 | 3.3 | 2.1 | 2.5 |
| Guyana | 0.4 | 0.4 | 0.3 | 0.3 | 0.2 |
| Trinidad and Tobago | 1.2 | 1.1 | 1.2 | 1.2 | 1.7 |
| EU (formerly EEC) | 30.8 | 29.0 | 27.7 | 24.7 | 22.5 |
| United Kingdom | 13.3 | 13.4 | 12.1 | 12.3 | 11.5 |
| Norway | 6.6 | 5.8 | 6.7 | 6.4 | 9.1 |
| Japan | 2.2 | 2.3 | 1.3 | 1.8 | 2.3 |
| United States | 36.8 | 33.4 | 40.9 | 37.0 | 39.1 |
| Venezuela | 0.1 | 0.1 | 0.0 | 0.0 | 0.0 |
| Others | 7.9 | 12.1 | 8.6 | 17.0 | 14.2 |

Source: World Bank and Statistical Institute of Jamaica.

OECD INVESTMENT POLICY REVIEWS – ISBN 92-64-10509-3 – © OECD 2004

Table 2.8. **Imports from principal trading partners**
In percentage of total imports

|  | 1996 | 1997 | 1998 | 1999 | 2000 |
|---|---|---|---|---|---|
| Canada | 3.0 | 3.0 | 3.2 | 3.3 | 3.1 |
| CARICOM | 10.0 | 10.1 | 10.4 | 10.7 | 11.1 |
| Guyana | 0.2 | 0.7 | 1.0 | 1.0 | 1.0 |
| Trinidad and Tobago | 8.5 | 7.8 | 7.7 | 9.8 | 10.0 |
| EU (formerly EEC) | 11.0 | 12.8 | 9.6 | 3.8 | 3.8 |
| United Kingdom | 3.9 | 3.7 | 3.8 | 3.2 | 3.1 |
| Netherland Antilles | 0.3 | 0.4 | 0.2 | 0.8 | 0.4 |
| Japan | 5.6 | 6.9 | 6.7 | 6.1 | 6.0 |
| United States | 52.2 | 48.1 | 50.9 | 48.5 | 44.8 |
| Venezuela | 2.3 | 2.1 | 1.5 | 1.8 | 3.9 |
| Others | 15.6 | 16.6 | 17.5 | 25.0 | 27.0 |

*Source:* World Bank and Statistical Institute of Jamaica.

Traditional products such as bauxite, alumina and sugar still account for the bulk of Jamaican exports. More specifically, crude materials represented 51.2 per cent of all Jamaican exports in 2001, whereas food at 15.5 per cent and free zone exports at 13.5 per cent were the other two most important items. On the import side, machinery and transport equipment at 25 per cent, mineral fuels at 16.5 per cent, food at 13.5 per cent, manufactured goods at 13.2 per cent were the main import goods. Imports from free zones accounted for 3.8 per cent of all Jamaican imports in 2001.

## 2.6. Investment regime

All investment related activities in Jamaica are governed by general legislation. Jamaican law does not provide for a legal and regulatory framework specifically applicable to foreign direct investment. In fact, foreign investment is not defined as such in domestic legislation, albeit it is protected under common law and by legislation related to investment incentives. Moreover, Jamaica does not apply any screening process for foreign investors, as was the case before the country liberalized its investment regime at the beginning of the 1990s. Very few barriers to the right to establish a business exist for foreign investors. Most restrictions are with respect to work permits and visa requirements. Some restrictions may take the form of higher minimum capital requirements such as in the banking sector. In other cases, discrimination could be exercised in the application of registration and licensing requirements in a number of services sectors.[12]

Table 2.9. **Goods exports and imports**

In percentage

| | Exports (2000) | Imports (2000) | Exports (2001) | Imports (2001) |
|---|---|---|---|---|
| **Total goods exports** | **100.0** | **100.0** | **100.0** | **100.0** |
| General merchandise exports | 83.2 | | 84.4 | |
| General merchandise imports | | 94.8 | | 95.3 |
| Food | 14.6 | 12.8 | 15.5 | 13.5 |
| Beverages and tobacco | 3.8 | 0.8 | 3.3 | 0.9 |
| Crude materials | 47.2 | 1.5 | 51.2 | 1.3 |
| Mineral fuels | 0.2 | 18.6 | 1.4 | 16.5 |
| Animal and vegetable oils | 0.0 | 0.6 | 0.0 | 0.5 |
| Chemicals | 4.5 | 10.8 | 4.4 | 10.7 |
| Manufactured goods | 0.8 | 12.7 | 0.7 | 13.2 |
| Machinery and transport equipment | 1.7 | 21.6 | 1.1 | 25.0 |
| Miscellaneous manufactured goods | 10.4 | 12.9 | 6.8 | 11.2 |
| Miscellaneous commodities | 0.0 | 2.5 | 0.0 | 2.5 |
| Free zone exports | 14.3 | | 13.5 | |
| Free zone imports | | 4.1 | | 3.8 |
| Goods procured in ports | 2.5 | 1.1 | 2.1 | 0.9 |

*Source:* Statistical Institute of Jamaica.

The Government of Jamaica has no restrictions on the movement of foreign currencies flowing either into or out of Jamaica. This facilitates the free movement of capital to other countries, whether for investment or repatriation purposes.

The right of property is upheld in the Constitution, subject to a few limitations. Expropriation of lands may take place under the Land Acquisitions Act, which provides compensation on the basis of market value. With the exception of free zones, foreign investment profits are subject to a 25 per cent tax rate for individuals and 33⅓ per cent for companies under the Income Tax Act. Dividends are subject to the applicable rate of 25 per cent or 33 1/3 per cent withholding tax.

The Government of Jamaica offers a number of investment incentives through various pieces of legislation. Some of these incentives falls under the definition of export subsidies, as defined by the WTO in its Agreement on Subsidies and Countervailing Duties (SCM), and will therefore need to be eliminated by the end of 2007.[13] In February 2003, Dr. Paul Robertson, Jamaica's Minister of Development, announced that the Government was spearheading legislation aimed at revising the incentive scheme regimes. The Government is working in collaboration with USAID and the Jamaica Chamber of Commerce on the *Jamaica Regulations Legislation and Process Improvement Project*. The intent is to look at the legislative framework, regulations and the

OECD INVESTMENT POLICY REVIEWS – ISBN 92-64-10509-3 – © OECD 2004

administrative practices, which impinge on the efforts at ensuring that incentives can be properly applied and effectively implemented. The Development Minister however emphasized, that any new incentive system had to be applied in a non-discriminatory manner to both local and foreign investors and allow for continuing assessment of the effectiveness of these incentive packages.

Under the Jamaica Companies Act, investors are generally required either to establish a local company, or to register a branch office of a foreign-owned enterprise. Branches of companies incorporated abroad must register with the Registrar of Companies within a month of their establishment in Jamaica. Applications for incentive benefits must be made to JAMPRO, the Jamaican Government agency responsible for promoting and processing investment proposals.

## Agricultural incentives

### Approved farmer status

The farmer that engages in the production of certain crops qualifies for "approved farmer" status and the ensuing benefits. Activities qualifying include:

- Most agricultural products grown and produced in Jamaica.
- Companies involved in the hatching of eggs.

The successful attainment of 'approved farmer' status guarantees the farmer income tax and import duty concessions for up to ten years, after which the status may be renewed.

## Film, music and entertainment incentives

### Motion picture encouragement act

A "recognized film producer" is entitled to:

- Relief from income tax for a period not exceeding nine (9) years from the date of the first release of the motion picture.
- An investment allowance of 70 per cent of the expenditure on the facilities, which may be carried forward beyond the initial nine (9) year period, is also granted for income tax purposes.
- Exemption from the payment of import duty on equipment, machinery and materials for the building of studios or for use in motion picture production.

## Manufacturing incentives

### Export industry encouragement act

To qualify for incentives under this act the manufacturer must be an exporter of manufactured products. In the case of a full exporter (that is, 100 per cent of the goods manufactured are exported), the business must be designed to export manufactured products in exchange for hard currencies (therefore, the CARICOM market is not usually the focus of this exporter). In the case of a partial exporter, producers must export a threshold of 5 per cent of their production to non-CARICOM markets.

Having fulfilled these requirements the manufacturer may receive concessions on income tax for ten (10) years as well as exemption from import duties on raw materials and machinery. The income tax rebate is granted according to the percentage of export profits to total profits. For new exporters, the rebate is calculated based on percentage of export sales to total sales, while for the already existing exporter, the rebate is calculated based on incremental export sales over a base year. The Act has been amended to provide benefits where incremental exports to non-CARICOM countries are in excess of 5 per cent of total exports.

### Bauxite and alumina industries encouragement act

Under this Act, if a business is engaged in the mining of bauxite or the production of alumina in Jamaica they are automatically qualified for import duty concessions on capital goods, lubricating oils, grease and other chemicals.

### Petroleum refinery encouragement act

A registered oil refiner may import articles for the construction and operation of the refinery as well as for the purpose of manufacturing petroleum products duty free. Furthermore, the manufacturer is exempt from paying income tax, or tax on dividends paid to shareholders, for a period of up to seven (7) years after which he has six (6) years to carry forward net losses incurred during that period.

## Tourism incentives

### Hotel incentives act

For a hotel to benefit from this Act they must contain ten (10) or more bedrooms as well as facilities for meals and the accommodation of transient guests, including tourists. The Act offers income tax relief and duty concessions for up to fifteen (15) years for convention-type hotels (hotels with at least 350 bedrooms), and ten (10) years for regular hotels.

OECD INVESTMENT POLICY REVIEWS – ISBN 92-64-10509-3 – © OECD 2004

### Resort cottages act

The resort cottage must contain at least two (2) furnished bedrooms with kitchen, living room and bathroom facilities, used for the accommodation of transient guests including tourists, in order to qualify for reward. In this case, the business receives income tax relief for up to seven (7) years as well as duty free importation of building materials and furnishings.

## Manufacturing/information technology incentives

### Jamaica export free zone act

Before a manufacturer can take advantage of the concessions made available by this Act, they have to ensure that all transactions must be conducted in US currency in addition to the fact that they are actually located within the free zone area. However, some firms outside of the free zone area may be allowed to benefit under the single entity free zone incentive. To get single entity free-zone status, a company must:

- be registered according to the provisions of the Companies Act;
- export at least 85 per cent of its production; and
- receive an approval from the Bank of Jamaica.

The "free-zone" status enables manufacturers and service providers (in the case of informatics free zones) to benefit from the exemption from income tax on profits as well as import duties and licensing. Furthermore, there exists a special provision under this Act, which permits the repatriation of foreign exchange by overseas investors to its parent company without any form of recourse on the part of the Government.

### Accelerated depreciation/special capital allowance

Qualified businesses must be certified by the Ministry of Industry, Commerce and Technology. For data processing/system development businesses, at least 20 per cent of its gross income must be derived from exports. Upon qualification, a certified business is granted a special allowance of capital expenditure for:

- 50 per cent of the full cost of any new machinery in the year of purchase; and
- a further 50 per cent in the 2nd year.

## Incentives that apply to all industries

### Industry incentives act

If the business is a producer of an "approved product" which has a supply market of less than 60 per cent of the demand market, then they may gain "approved enterprise" status and thus, stand to benefit from this Act. This exempts them from the payment of income tax for a period of time, depending on the product.

### Foreign sales corporation (FSC) act

An FSC is a foreign sales corporation, which is allowed to earn some tax exemption on its exports to the United States. This Act provides relief from the Common External Tariff and the General Consumption Tax on equipment, machinery and materials coming into the country. In addition, it provides for up to five years income tax relief.

### International financial companies act

In an effort to promote offshore banking facilities, Government has provided international financial companies with income tax relief on both profits and capital gains.

### Shipping act

Once a company is recognized as an "approved Shipping Corporation" they may receive tax relief and concessions on import duties for up to ten (10) years.

### Moratorium on duties

This is granted to companies which do not qualify under existing incentives laws yet have the potential to contribute significantly to foreign exchange earnings, employment, and so on. If the company is able to prove that it holds this potential, it may be granted relief from import duties for up to three years by the Minister of Finance.

### Modernization of industry

To qualify under this incentive program the investor must provide necessary support, service, or raw material, to export manufacturer(s); or, be involved in export trade or plan to enter the export market. This will guarantee them relief from the General Consumption Tax levied on capital goods.

### Urban renewal act

This Act is targeted at persons or organisations that facilitate or carry out urban development in depressed areas. Relief from income tax, stamp duty and transfer tax is given to those persons who engage in transactions geared towards urban development.

### Factory construction law

This law focuses on companies who construct factories and lease or sell them to manufacturers under the Export Industry Encouragement Act. It grants relief from:

- import duties for items which are not available locally; and
- income tax on income from factory leasing or gains made from sales.

### Bilateral investment and double taxation treaties

In addition to the incentives packages, Jamaica has signed several bilateral investment treaties (Argentina, China, Cuba, Egypt, France, Germany, Indonesia, Italy, the Netherlands, Switzerland, the United Kingdom, the United States, and Zimbabwe) to improve the business environment and provide legal certainty to the investor. It has also signed double taxation treaties with Canada, CARICOM, China, Denmark, Germany, Israel, Norway, Sweden, Switzerland, the United Kingdom, and the United States.

## 2.7. Investment promotion agency: Jamaica promotions corporation (JAMPRO)

JAMPRO was created in 1988 as a way to consolidate into a single body all the functions related to investment promotion and facilitation. In 1990, while housed within the Ministry of Development, Planning and Production, the JAMPRO Act was passed in Parliament, establishing the company as a statutory body of the Government of Jamaica. Today, JAMPRO functions under the Ministry of Development and its mandate and services have become more facilitatory, while focusing primarily on investment and export promotion within the Leisure, Manufacturing, Agribusiness and Information Technology sectors.

JAMPRO develops and implements programs to encourage, expand and diversify investments; modernize production and management systems of companies; and stimulate growth of exports from Jamaica. These programs are designed to meet the needs of the entrepreneur in business development from project idea through to implementation and beyond. JAMPRO provides information on Jamaica's investment opportunities, economic and market trends, as well as cost models and data on various types of investment.

JAMPRO's focus is to support the development of businesses in:

- Leisure Industry – Tourism, Film and Music.
- Manufacturing and Mining.
- Agriculture and Agro-industry.
- Information Technology and International Business.

JAMPRO also facilitates various types of Government approvals on behalf of investors, including the following:

- Approval for incentives as applicable.
- Film and mining licenses.
- Work permits and visas.
- Land and building approvals.
- Other approvals.

With respect to joint venture partnerships, JAMPRO assists investors by:

- Evaluating project proposals.
- Preparing internationally acceptable business profiles.
- Identifying joint venture partners and offering matchmaking services for investors seeking cooperation in the areas of capital, technology, management, marketing and training.
- Advising and participating in the negotiation of joint ventures.
- Identifying sources of financial assistance and endorsing projects for funding.

JAMPRO provides assistance with the identification of appropriate sites (land and factory space) for projects. It can also assists with all aspects of film production, including:

- Provision of a comprehensive service for all film makers in production or location scouting.
- Provision of incentives for production companies.

Business enterprises can benefit from technical assistance sourced by JAMPRO from bilateral and multilateral agencies. JAMPRO also provides counterpart staff to help with:

- in-plant consultancy;
- advice on production methods and equipment selection;
- plant design and layout.

JAMPRO provides the secretariat for both the Trade Facilitation and Investment Facilitation Boards. The Trade Facilitation Board, a private and public sector grouping, is responsible for ensuring that exporters are afforded an opportunity to have their trade concerns/problems considered and resolved. The Investment Facilitation Board, comprising of members from the public sector, seeks to resolve any problem arising during the investment process and to expedite the granting of the necessary Government approvals.

JAMPRO also registers all exporters. There is an annual registration fee. The register provides current data on exporters, their bona fides and ability to carry out their declared activities. It provides market intelligence and assistance with product promotion in order to help exporters locate and penetrate overseas markets.

JAMPRO is also committed to the development of new market areas through overseas-funded business development programs such as the European Union-funded Trade Development Project, and projects through the Caribbean Export Development Agency (CEDA) and the Centre for the Development of Enterprises (CDE).

JAMPRO is strategically located in New York, London and Toronto, to serve business interests. The activities at these offices include:

● Processing trade enquiries that emanate from overseas sources.

● Promotions such as arranging incoming and outgoing trade missions, direct sales visits to companies, in-store promotions and representing Jamaican companies at trade fairs.

● Conducting market surveys and research to identify export opportunities.

ISBN 92-64-10509-3
OECD Investment Policy Reviews
Caribbean Rim: Costa Rica, Dominican Republic and Jamaica
© OECD 2004

Chapter 3

# Investor Perceptions

Investor perceptions of Jamaica as a prime location for FDI are improving. They are generally supportive of the Jamaican Government's efforts to attract FDI. Political stability and democratic Government rank high among the factors that draw investors to Jamaica. Investors also recognize that Jamaica's geographical proximity to North America, in particular easy air and shipping connections to Miami, good telecommunication services, and a qualified English-speaking workforce are major assets contributing to invite foreigners to invest in Jamaica. In the case of export-oriented investors, preferential market access to the United States under the Caribbean Basin Initiative (CBI) and the Caribbean Basin Trade Partnership Act (CBTPA), as well as to other Caribbean countries under the soon-to-be-fully-implemented CARICOM Single Market and Economy are important considerations. Overall trade liberalization within the Free Trade Area of the Americas (FTAA) process will also provide foreign investors with additional market opportunities.

Certain areas can be improved to further enhance Jamaica's investment climate. Investors express concern on labor issues, particularly on difficult management-labor relations in some industries. This reflects the need to refocus investment promotion strategy on knowledge-intensive industries that value workers as productive assets. The implementation of productivity incentive programs, coupled with greater flexibility in workweeks, would bring added productivity gains. Another factor that investors perceive to be detrimental to their investments is the high cost of utilities and especially the high cost of petroleum. Electric power is generated from imported fuel oil, which partly explains the higher costs. Yet the cost of the utility should be significantly reduced with adequate investment and modernization of facilities following the privatization of Jamaica Public Service Company (JPSCo). Transaction costs are also identified to be relatively high. Investors are stressing the need to minimize bureaucratic business approval procedures. Lastly, there are perceived social costs to doing investment in Jamaica, particularly in Kingston, due to problems in personal safety, as well as in security. This issue might be partially addressed by increasing security measures at business facilities and residences.

In a study conducted with twenty-nine existing or potential investors in Jamaica in August 1998, the US Department of Commerce highlighted three primary challenges identified by foreign investors.[14] The need to modernize infrastructure services topped the list of concerns, traffic congestion, poor urban and inter-city roads, and inadequate mass transit. The reliability of electricity and telecommunication services was also singled out. These two sectors have since then undergone major changes and benefited greatly from an influx of foreign direct investment, following the privatization and liberalization in each of these sectors, respectively. Crime and lack of security came second as challenges facing foreign investors. Personal safety as well as safety against pilferage were of particular concerns. Finally, labor issues were mentioned as having a negative impact on the overall investment climate. Traditionally, management-labor relations have been quite difficult in certain industries, as demonstrated by the number of strikes in recent years. However, the recommendations contained in the 1994 Labour Market Reform Committee report, which included modernizing the island's labor laws, implementing flexible work arrangements and restructuring the Ministry of Labour to make it better able to deal with industrial relations disputes, have yet to be fully implemented. The process of labor market reform is on going in the country. In January 2002, the National Labour Market Information System was launched as a tool to improve the flow of information to users on demand and supply side of the labor market.

## 3.1. Recommendations

Before the next plenary meeting of the Caribbean Rim Investment Initiative, a number of concrete measures should be implemented by the Government of Jamaica, with the support of international organisations such as the Inter-American Development Bank and the Organization for Economic Cooperation and Development (OECD), to improve the investment climate in the country. These measures should include:

a) the review of tax regulations to identify inefficiencies in statutes and procedures, and the strengthening of Jamaica's Double Taxation Treaty network, which does not include major investors such as France, Ireland, and Spain; and

b) the review of work permit procedures and business visas to facilitate greater access for key personnel related to investment projects.

Moreover, cognizant of the need to eliminate export subsidy programs such as free zones under the WTO Agreement on Subsidies and Countervailing Duties by the end of 2007, Jamaica should also carry out:

c) a review, as announced in February 2003, of its investment-related incentive packages, using a cost-benefit analysis to assess the use and provision of such incentives in the country.

With a view to encouraging linkages between foreign and local investors, Jamaica should undertake:

d) the establishment of a clearing house where small and medium-sized local companies meeting some well-defined standards of performance would register and could become suppliers of the foreign (and local) companies operating in free zones. Such a mechanism would encourage backward linkages; and

e) the establishment of an annual employment survey and assessment of economic inputs to monitor the progress in employment and linkages arising from FDI so as to use these results in shaping future policy.

Initiatives such as the recent IADB-financed e-government loan, which offers some 900 Jamaicans partial funding for high-level professional training in information and communication technology should be replicated and encouraged. As the country is targeting the ICT sector and telecommunications, Jamaica should review:

f) its investment in training and re-training programs aimed at improving the technological skills of its workforce with a view to increasing the competitive advantage of the country as a knowledge economy. In particular, Jamaica should undertake a full review of skills needed for the future and skills presently available so as to measure and address the gap with skills training, skills upgrading, and conversion programs.

Jamaica would also greatly benefit from:

g) the establishment of an annual benchmark survey of investors views on critical issues affecting investment decisions.

Reducing crime should remain one of the Government's top priorities, although it is worth noting that the real impact of violent crimes on FDI is difficult to assess since tourists and foreign business people are rarely the victims of such acts. Nevertheless, there is no doubt that it contributes to deter foreign investment. The Government is addressing this major problem and has recently adopted a multifaceted approach to strengthen and reorganize the police force and improve the country's access to the justice system.

# Notes

1. See Department of Commerce, Jamaica: Investor Attitude Study, August 1998, at *http://usembassy.state.gov/kingston/wwwhfjia.html*.

2. Francis, Patricia. *Recent Trends and Policy Development in the Caribbean Region: The Case of Jamaica*, April 5, 2001.

3. For more detail on the market structure of the Jamaican economy, see Planning Institute of Jamaica, *Economic and Social Survey 2001*, April 25, 2002, (*www.pioj.gov.jm*).

4. The fiscal year begins on April 1.

5. There are three types of secondary schools in Jamaica: traditional, vocational and technical. Traditional high schools focus their curriculum around academics, whereas vocational and technical high schools emphasize the skill-training aspect of the curriculum. Enrollment in secondary technical schools increased by more than 400 per cent between 1990 and 2000.

6. *www.jftc.com/news&publications/Statistics/statistics.htm*.

7. Jamaica has also signed a bilateral textiles and apparel agreement with the United States and Canada within the context of the WTO Agreement on Textiles and Clothing.

8. The founding members were: Barbados, Guyana, Jamaica, and Trinidad and Tobago. The Bahamas, Belize, Dominica, Grenada, Montserrat, St. Lucia, and St. Vincent and the Grenadines acceded in May 1974. Antigua and Barbuda and St. Kitts and Nevis joined in July 1974, while Suriname joined July 4, 1995. Haiti became an official member in July 2002 after having ratified the Treaty. The Bahamas is an associate but not a full member of the Common Market.

9. CARICOM members have yet to ratify the Revised Treaty and enact it into domestic law.

10. The Framework Agreement was signed on August 22, 1998 and the Protocol to Implement the Agreement Establishing the Free Trade Area between CARICOM and the Dominican Republic was signed on April 28, 2000.

11. The Agreement was signed by the Chairman of the Conference of CARICOM Heads of Government and the Minister of Economic and International Affairs of Cuba at the twenty-first conference of Heads of Government of the Caribbean Community in July 2000.

12. An inventory of non-conforming measures (*i.e.* discriminatory) measures is being prepared by Jamaica in the context of the Caribbean Rim Investment Initiative.

13. At their Ministerial Meeting held in Qatar in November 2001, WTO members agreed to postpone to the end of 2007 the elimination of export or local content subsidies by developing countries under the SCM Agreement. Export subsidies were to be eliminated by 2003.

14. See Department of Commerce, Jamaica: Investor Attitude Study, August 1998, at *http://usembassy.state.gov/kingston/wwwhfjia.html*.

OECD PUBLICATIONS, 2, rue André-Pascal, 75775 PARIS CEDEX 16
PRINTED IN FRANCE
(14 2004 02 1 P) ISBN 92-64-10509-3 – No. 53327 2004